sam hunt

backroads

CHARTING A POET'S LIFE

I'm too far out
                    out here
I'm too far out for
                         anyone
                                  to reach,
please, tay.

sam hunt

backroads

CHARTING A POET'S LIFE

craig potton publishing

First published in 2009 by Craig Potton Publishing
98 Vickerman Street, PO Box 555, Nelson 7040, New Zealand
www. craigpotton.co.nz

ISBN 978 1 877517 05 1

Printed in China by Midas Printing International Ltd

contents

foreword

This book is based on transcripts that followed many conversations I had with Sam Hunt during 2008 and 2009. They came about because I was intrigued by the quite singular and unique path he has followed—forty years of living off his wits as a poet, putting poems in front of audiences decade after decade, and always championing the poem as a living, breathing thing that demands to be taken out from beyond the covers of a book.

Originally it was intended that this book should be published in 2008, but we decided that *Doubtless,* his volume of new and selected poems, should come first. When Sam initially raised the possibility of *Doubtless,* I made it very clear that poetry was not an area of my expertise. His response, which forever endeared him to me, was an impassioned growl, 'No, that's good, that's good.' Sam, as he does with all his audiences, immediately gave me permission to listen to his poems on my own terms, to be comfortable making sense of them from within my own experience.

And indeed I am very grateful that I was able to immerse myself in so many of his poems before we began the conversations that have led to *Backroads.* For when everything is stripped back, arguably the most important thing you really need to know about Sam is the centrality of the poem in his life. The more we've talked, the more I've heard, and the more I've got to know him, it's always the poems that keep rising to the surface—they are, and will always be, the axis of this man's world.

The personal story of Sam Hunt is not the focus of this book—that task will be left to someone further down the line. This is a book in which he reflects on his life as a poet, I hope an illuminating glimpse down the long backroad that Sam chooses to travel.

Robbie Burton
Co-owner/Publisher
Craig Potton Publishing

Sam Hunt, Kaipara Harbour, 2009

to begin at the beginning

I've got a poem called 'Return in Spring' and it starts off:

> At war all day in the buffalo grass,
> Our backs would itch all night.

and then later on in the poem it says:

> I have no memories as others do
> Of family outings: we had it all here,

I certainly was gifted a garden of Eden to grow up in. In those days Milford Beach (on Auckland's North Shore) was still a very bachy sort of place which had a lot of quite eccentric people. It was a good place to be a child with the sea right there—we lived right by the sea—and I would describe my childhood as basically a very, very happy one.

I grew up with a lot of words, a lot of poems. I heard poems at an early stage, told by my father and mother and my grandfather, so poems as spoken things were quite natural. I don't think I was precocious, but I did know a lot of poems. It always seemed to me to be normal.

When my parents met, my father was forty-two and my mother was twelve; years later they got together, despite the thirty-year age difference. One of the main things our parents shared, apart from their love for each other and for us kids, was a love of words. Their taste was different—my mother would scoff at my father's taste in poetry—he was a fan of the big ballads. Dad used to say this particular poem, an early ballad by Thomas Campbell, 'Lord Ullin's Daughter', and I loved this poem, and I loved him saying it. I can remember, when I was about six or seven, asking him to say this poem while he was shaving one morning. He said, 'I haven't got time today, I haven't got time,' as he had to get the bus to work—my father was a lawyer who didn't have a car—and anyway, the next thing he is into the poem:

Betty Hunt with Sam, Milford Beach, late 1940s

Lord Ullin's Daughter

A chieftain to the Highlands bound
Cries, 'Boatman, do not tarry!
And I'll give thee a silver pound
To row us o'er the ferry.'

'Now, who be ye would cross Lochgyle,
This dark and stormy water?'
'Oh, I'm the chief of Ulva's isle,
And this Lord Ullin's daughter.

'And fast before her father's men
Three days we've fled together;
For, should he find us in the glen,
My blood would stain the heather.

'His horsemen hard behind us ride;
Should they our steps discover,
Then who would cheer my bonny bride
When they have slain her lover?'

Out spoke the hardy island wight,
'I'll go, my chief—I'm ready:—
It is not for your silver bright,
But for your winsome lady:

'And by my word, the bonny bird
In danger shall not tarry;
So, though the waves are raging white,
I'll row you o'er the ferry.'

By this the storm grew loud apace,
The water-wraith was shrieking,
And in the scowl of heaven each face
Grew dark as they were speaking.

But still as wilder blew the wind,
And as the night grew drearer,
Adown the glen rode armèd men,
Their trampling sounded nearer.

'Oh, haste thee, haste!' the lady cries;
'Though tempests round us gather,
I'll meet the raging of the skies,
But not an angry father.'

The boat has left a stormy land
A stormy sea before her,—
When, O! too strong for human hand
The tempest gathered o'er her.

And still they rowed amidst the roar
Of waters fast prevailing;
Lord Ullin reached that fatal shore,—
His wrath was changed to wailing.

For sore dismayed through storm and shade,
His child he did discover:
One lovely hand she stretched for aid,
And one was round her lover.

'Come back! come back!' he cried in grief,
'Across this stormy water;
And I'll forgive your Highland chief,
My daughter!—O my daughter!'

'Twas vain: the loud waves lashed the shore,
Return or aid preventing;
The waters wild went o'er his child,
And he was left lamenting.

[Thomas Campbell]

Of course he finished the whole poem and missed the bus. He got the next bus and I got the poem.

My mother's taste in poetry was pretty wide, eclectic is possibly the word for it—far-ranging certainly. I remember that my mum actually introduced me to James K. Baxter. She bought in 1962 a volume of Baxter's which had recently been published called *Howrah Bridge and other poems.* It came from the Minerva Bookshop—I've still got the copy with the side stamped 'Minerva Bookshop, Commerce Street,

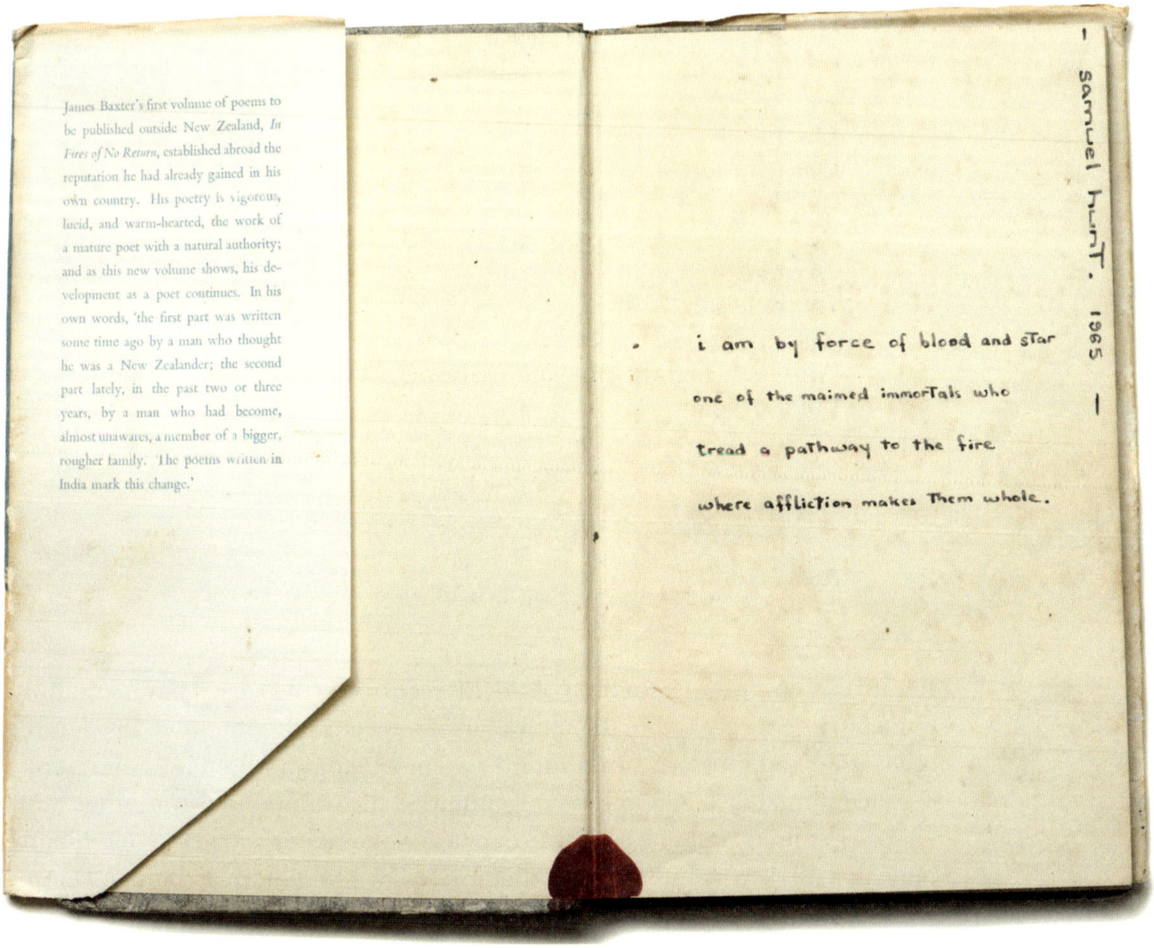

Sam Hunt's copy of Howrah Bridge and other poems, *by James K. Baxter*

Auckland'. I particularly liked 'Evidence at the Witch Trials', the reciting of which would eventually contribute to my expulsion from St Peter's College.

My grandfather Harry Bosworth would come down from the north—not very far from where I live these days—with poems. He used to quote a lot of my favourites—like A. E. Housman and Wilfred Owen—and I remember him quoting a poem of Dylan Thomas's:

In My Craft or Sullen Art

In my craft or sullen art
Exercised in the still night
When only the moon rages
And the lovers lie abed
With all their griefs in their arms,
I labour by singing light
Not for ambition or bread
Or the strut and trade of charms
On the ivory stages
But for the common wages
Of their most secret heart.

Not for the proud man apart
From the raging moon I write
On these spindrift pages
Not for the towering dead
With their nightingales and psalms
But for the lovers, their arms
Round the griefs of the ages,
Who pay no praise or wages
Nor heed my craft or art.

[Dylan Thomas]

After that my mum and I got hold of the LP recordings of Dylan Thomas reading his poems and we listened to them for years. I was eternally grateful to my mother because she had a bloody good sound system when everyone had radiograms. We called it the Black Box and it really pumped the sound out. My mother went to a lot of trouble and considerable expense to get it—it was very good-quality hi-fidelity (this was pre-stereo). We'd crank Dylan Thomas up so loud—'Do not go gentle into that good night' at full tilt—people walking along Milford Beach out in front would be thinking, 'What the hell's going on up there.'

Some people express surprise when they come here and realise how much classical music I listen to. I don't know why they're surprised but they are. They might say, 'Well, how do you get into it?' I feel like saying, 'Well, how do you get into a cup of tea? You pour it.' My father had a lot to do with classical music. He was fairly marinated in the great composers. I remember one night coming home from a concert with my father at the Auckland Town Hall—there was a French cellist, Paul Tortelier, playing with what was then called the National Orchestra, and they played Dvořák, which I'd never heard (I was ten at the time) and it just knocked me out of my chair. Afterwards we were walking down Queen Street and we met Dad's old friend Lewis Eady standing outside his record shop. It was closed down for the night, but he opened up the shop and we got a copy of the Dvořák—it wasn't Paul Tortelier's version but another one by Pierre Fournier.

Percy Hunt

We caught the last ferry across to the North Shore and got back to Milford Beach where our sound system was waiting, and we played the Dvořák Cello Concerto until the sun came up over the Coromandel. I've done that many times since and often think of my father and all those things combining, and my mother being quirky enough to go off and get this system; she wasn't a snob but I don't think she liked the sound of the old stereogram.

I got on very well with my father. I don't know that he ever got on so well with my two older brothers. In those days he was a busier man, even though by the time I came along he was sixty and still working as a lawyer because there was still financial pressure—he never made much money. Most of the people he represented could never pay him because they didn't have any money. He was a bloody good lawyer, a good barrister and a kind and compassionate man. Martyn Finlay, Justice Minister under the Norman Kirk Government, used to reckon that Percy Hunt was the best court advocate he had ever heard.

I have a letter from my father reacting to some of my poems. He talks about how I must think him a rum dad. He says:

> 'You no doubt feel that I'm a rum sort of father as illustrated by one of the three poems you read on 1YC on Tuesday night. I had of course read it myself some time ago and formed the impression that it rather stressed the filial at the expense of the paternal point of view.'

He goes on to say, 'I liked your poem and enjoyed your rendering of it.' That was written on 25 July 1971 so the poem must have been 'My Father Scything':

My Father Scything

My father was sixty when I was born,
twice my mother's age. But he's never been
around very much, neither at the mast
round the world; nor when I wanted him most.
He was somewhere else, like in his upstairs
Dickens-like law office counting the stars;
Or sometimes out with his scythe on Sunday
Working the path through the lupins toward the sea.

And the photograph album I bought myself
On leaving home, lies open on the shelf
At the one photograph I have of him,
My father scything. In the same album
Beside him, one of my mother.
I stuck them there on the page together.

It would have hurt, but it never occurred to me at the time that he would have been hurt by that.

A nurse came up to me one day after a show and said, 'I nursed your father when he was dying and he kept on saying this poem about time not saying anything.'

Time will say nothing but I told you so,
Time only knows the price we have to pay;
If I could tell you I would let you know.

It was Auden's 'If I Could Tell You'. Dad obviously loved that poem—it came from Mum—so he wasn't just left with the ballads. Some of those great lyric poems were part of his arsenal too.

There were conflicts at times between my parents, often exacerbated by the age difference, and as my father got older that age difference seemed to increase. I had a great relationship with both my mother and father. We talked about a lot of things. I'd sometimes go over and meet my father at his law office, we'd go and have dinner at a little restaurant called La Corvette, and then we'd catch the ferry home and talk about all sorts of things. Same with my mother. For a couple of such distinctive individuals they did a bloody good job, I reckon.

My parents weren't big social people—they didn't have parties as such—but somehow people would just congregate and end up at our house after drinking at the Mon Desir hotel, The Mon, now a block of hideous apartments. I can remember a number of poets who had a bit to do with my parents—Rex Fairburn, R. A. K. Mason and, before my birth, Robin Hyde. When Fairburn was at our place with his good old friend Clifton Firth, there was a lot of poetry and banter. They were always good Friday nights, often impromptu. Rex Fairburn was very fond of my mother, and I remember him chasing her over the roof. He was a very loud and colourful character—much liked and a great poet. There has always been, somewhere, a suggestion that his poem 'A Farewell' was addressed to my mother. I don't know whether that's true, and I've got no way of finding out. It makes no difference; it's a wonderful poem.

Apart from my parents, there were many other people who put poems in front of me. There's a poem by Charles Kingsley that my Aunt Hilary (my mum's younger sister) used to say—terribly out of date and out of fashion—called 'The Sands of Dee':

The Sands of Dee

'O Mary, go and call the cattle home,
            And call the cattle home,
            And call the cattle home
      Across the sands of Dee';
The western wind was wild and dank with foam,
      And all alone went she.

The western tide crept up along the sand,
            And o'er and o'er the sand,
            And round and round the sand,
      As far as eye could see.
The rolling mist came down and hid the land:
      And never home came she.

'Oh! is it weed, or fish, or floating hair—
            A tress of golden hair,
            A drownèd maiden's hair
      Above the nets at sea?
Was never salmon yet that shone so fair
      Among the stakes on Dee.'

They rowed her in across the rolling foam,
            The cruel, crawling foam,

The cruel, hungry foam,
To her grave beside the sea:
But still the boatmen hear her call the cattle home
Across the sands of Dee.

[Charles Kingsley]

Aunt Hilary was one of those people who throw the mirror out and she did that for me, just flashed me with a mirror of a poem in the sun, like a bright stone on the bank of a South Island river.

And so too, did my grandparents.

I grew up with the knowledge that my grandmother Elsa had been engaged to Joyce Cary, the Anglo-Irish novelist. Along came the First World War, and Cary went off to fight as an officer. In the meantime Elsa met someone who hadn't gone to fight for King and Country, Harry Bosworth. We had always heard that Mum was conceived out of wedlock under a rose bush at a garden party. However, what we learned later is that Joyce came back from the war, got together with Elsa, she conceived, but then something went awry and maybe he didn't know about the baby. Part of the deal set by Elsa's father (old Banks, the Chairman of the London Stock Exchange) was that Harry married Elsa and adopted Betty as his daughter. We didn't know anything about any of this—though Mum might have—until about ten years ago when a scholar from Cambridge, who was an expert on Joyce Cary, got hold of Mum. In her study of Cary she discovered that he had had an illegitimate daughter—my mother, Betty—prior to his being married and having his own family.

I did have an amazing connection with the Cary thing, long before I knew he could be my grandfather. In 1959 I heard, on the radio, a piece of very early electronic music, which was a setting of the great twentieth century Spanish poet García Lorca's 'Lament for the Death of a Bullfighter', written for his friend Ignacio Sánchez Mejías. Without sounding too melodramatic hearing this poem and the music was a big moment, one of the big ones, and it had something to do with putting me in the direction I went. I've always remembered its echoing lines in translation

at five in the afternoon.
Death laid eggs in the wound
at five in the afternoon.
At five in the afternoon.
At five o'clock in the afternoon.

It turned out that the music was written by Tristram Cary, who was a pioneering composer of electronic music, and none other than Joyce Cary's son. If the Cary story is true then, he would have turned out to be my mother's half-brother, and my uncle.

So Harry and Elsa came to New Zealand. Mum was born in England, coming out here when she was nine with her younger siblings, Imogen, Joan and Rowley; Hilary was born in New Zealand. Elsa and Harry separated in the 1940s.

Harry Bosworth

My grandfather Harry Bosworth had a phenomenal memory for poetry. Allen Curnow remembered his first meeting with Harry Bosworth—they later became friends—on the ferry going across to the North Shore, as there was this man, 'many sheets to the wind', hanging onto the flagpole reciting canto after canto of Byron's 'Don Juan'. Curnow could not get over how this drunk man, who was obviously not learned-looking could know such obscure verses, and so many of them.

Harry was a popular and well-known journalist on both the *Auckland Star* and the *New Zealand Herald*, and for many years he wrote a daily column which was widely read called 'Man About Town'. Harry was sacked from the *Herald* more than anybody in the history of the newspaper, but one time he also got sacked from the *Star* across the gully in Shortland Street for being drunk on the job. He often used to write up meetings that never took place.

Harry wasn't a great father—a good bloke on the ferry with his mates but not good on the domestic front. My mother would have nothing or as little as possible to do with him—too many bad memories. She was often called 'blue' at school because of the bruises she carried from his night-time rages. However, I always got on with old Harry—he had mellowed by the time I got to know him. The Harry Bosworth of 'A Purple Balloon', the poem I wrote about him, is a very different man from the one my mother knew and feared.

A Purple Balloon

1
As father to five children
they say he failed. His drinking
whisky for a week non-stop,
at every gulp, blinking,

at the wonder of it all,
the same blue eyes my mother
sometimes says she sees in me.
My grandfather was, they say,
a failure of the first degree.

And every Christmas Day, our
drunk old Santa Claus, he came.
With a pohutukawa
flower stuck like a clotted bloom
of blood on his coat lapel:
pockets full: always his green
bottle with its latch-on cap;
singing with us kids till all
we could do was yell and clap ...

The last Christmas he came he
gave me a purple balloon.

When turned twelve I hitch-hiked
north to Waiotu: run-down
farms and eroded hills; clay,
skylines gaping red with clay;
spending Easter with him in
his shack of fibrolite and tin:
for the three days drinking wine
he'd crushed from grape and let
ferment in an old tin can ...

Hangover sun and Sunday,
songs and a purple balloon.

2
When gangrene set in, my
grandfather's feet on a rack,
laid in a hospital bed
he watched them slowly turn black.
But even after they'd cut
both his legs to the knee, still
he claimed he could twitch his toes
and would ask for flowers at night
and what they'd done with his shoes.

Waiting the priest, no one
seemed to know quite what to do.

My mum watched the empty pit.
Hands behind their backs, the grave-
diggers wore white denim coats.
And after the priest had come
and gone, and the white men slid
the coffin down, we all dropped
paper poppies on the lid...

I tried to believe but couldn't
forget the purple balloon.

Drinking all day in this far
north harbour pub, I couldn't
help think of him, now dead. With
salt and whisky on his breath,
some sand-barred sailor locals
here still talk about, who stalks
the sand-bar singing where he
drowned one night: drunk, rolling
drunk on whisky down the bar...

I couldn't help but think of his
night; and a purple balloon.

When I was about twelve I expressed a wish to get to know him. Mum was very good—despite her own feelings towards him, she knew he'd mellowed and she let me go up and meet him north of Whangarei, where he was living (squatting, I might add, not renting, nothing respectable for Harry) in a large house which had become known as Chateau Boz, as in Bosworth. When I arrived at the house I knocked on the door and a head poked out from upstairs and it was Harry, who of course I'd met and remembered from visits to the family house: 'Hello Sam, hello Sam,' he said. 'Come on through—there's a horse downstairs, watch out for the horse, he's very friendly,' and then this horse walked out the front door.

He recognised a love of words in me and that was very much a part of our connection. I'd show him poems—when I look back on it I feel shame-faced, they were such gawky poems—but he was always incredibly encouraging. I remember showing him a couple I'd had in the school magazine. One of them was called 'Myself when young and dead', the other one—which won a prize—was called 'Child and Crucifix'. For all the fact that the poems rambled and had more than lots of great big adjectives—the flowery stuff of youth—they had a sound to them. One of the first poems of mine that Harry ever really did praise was called 'Spun

Quartered Moon'. It's got the line that I like: 'We watched as the horse shoe bay rose to the horse shoed moon'.

When Chateau Boz was demolished he moved further north from Whangarei to a place called Waiotu. He was a bit of a star in his way—people knew him. Many years after he was dead I walked into the pub that Harry would go to at Hukerenui, just north of Waiotu, and I said to the barman, 'A jug of beer please.' A woman, who turned out to be the barman's wife, poked her head through from the bottlestore and said, 'Christ's sake! I thought that was Harry Bosworth.' I said, 'Well I'm his grandson.' She said, 'You sound like him,' and that was about eight to ten years after his death.

My maternal grandmother was Elsa, and she died when I was about fourteen. She was great, and she was a poet too. She would never be described, even by the kindest critic, as a great poet nor would she have described herself that way, but she wrote some poems that have always stuck with me. There was one with the line 'And the waves breaking'—a refrain line that comes in at the end of each verse. When I wrote 'Wave Song' she was sort of there—present somewhere in that poem. She came from genteel literary stock. Her neighbours, when she grew up in Kensington Gardens in London, were the Sitwells—Osbert and Sacheverell and the famous Edith Sitwell, who wrote that wonderful poem 'Still Falls the Rain'. Elsa's mother's name goes back from Banks to Norton then back to Arnold—that's the connection with the Victorian poet Matthew Arnold—and they were in turn related to the Huxleys.

When the violence became too intense, Elsa left Harry—she couldn't take it anymore. They were living in Devonport, and Hilary was a baby. The night they left Elsa gathered the children together and got on the ferry. Mum knew they had enough money to get on a tram and to go to the end of the line, which was as far away from Harry as possible. They had the choice of going down the coast through St Heliers or up into the Ponsonby–Herne Bay area. They went to Herne Bay because it was the first tram that came. They went to the end of the line and found a boarding house. They went in—they had no money or very little money—and the man said, 'Oh, Mrs Bosworth, you're booked in.' They never knew how that had happened. Harry had no idea and he wouldn't have done it anyway if he had known. It was a completely random choice of where they went. Mum remembered that well.

At some point Elsa's father sent money through, but he was very careful who it went to. It didn't go to Harry or Elsa—it was money so that Betty and her brother and sisters could go to Catholic boarding schools, Mum and Imogen and Joan and Hilary later went to Sacré Coeur, which is now called Baradene. Poor old Rowley was sent on down to St Pat's Silverstream, which he absolutely hated—he had some terrible stories to tell from that. I'm guessing Mum was about twelve when

Elsa left Harry. She would still have been going to St Leo's Convent in Devonport, and that was one stable thing she had. She'd often go home and there'd be a note on the door to say they weren't living there anymore and they were living out at some other address. It was Depression time too—the whole thing must have been very bleak. In later years, when people got all romantic and dewy eyed about Devonport, the beautiful Devonport, Mum always said it represented for her a sort of hell on earth.

I benefitted from being the last of old loins, as they say in the Old Testament. I was sort of a privileged child. I don't think I was spoiled, but I was given more space—more space and grace. In later years my mother used to think back with horror at me, five years old, riding off on a two-wheeler, quarter-sized bicycle to Albany, which is a long way away. Some friend berated her: 'I saw Sam out on his bike on the main road,' and Mum said, 'But he rides to school.' I wouldn't let my eleven-year-old son out on the highway with his bike. It was a gentler world then.

I started school at Campbell's Bay Primary School, then when I was about six—it must have been the time that my mother thought that Catholicism was what she wanted to practise—Jonathan and I changed schools. I remember the day very well. We went from Campbell's Bay to St Joseph's Convent. Apart from one particularly sadistic nun, Sister Mary-Antony, it was a very good place—but a strange place. It was an orphanage as well as a Catholic school so there were orphaned kids and day kids like me, both girls and boys. Overall, for me it was a very happy time.

When I was in Standard Two at St Joseph's Convent (this was in 1954), my teacher was Sister Mary Bernadine—lovely woman, a large woman. One day she said something in class about poetry, maybe asked if anyone knew a poem. My hand went up. I said this poem, which I knew, which I'd heard my mother saying, by E. E. Cummings:

No Time Ago

no time ago
or else a life
walking in the dark
i met christ

jesus)my heart
flopped over
and lay still

while he passed(as

close as i'm to you
yes closer
made of nothing
except loneliness

[E. E. Cummings]

The next day Mum was in Milford and Sister Bernadine saw her and said, 'Mrs Hunt, Sammy got up and said this poem. I've never heard anything like it. It was lovely.' Sister Bernadine had even written the poem on the board, she liked it so much. I didn't remember that—Mum told me the story years later.

Poems hit me as a much more spiritual experience than my first communion or first confession—in terms of spirituality, they weren't even on the same mountainside as poems. I can't remember not loving poems, certain poems. They've always been central to my thinking.

From about age eight, I always imaged I would live as a poet. I wrote a poem when I was seven, a Christmas tree poem:

Climb up the cliff path to the pines
where through their needles salt winds blow
and far below the fish and ocean go
and down the cliff path home
bring one lone small Christmas tree
and by the beach let it in warm winds grow.

It's good rhythm, that last line—the rhythms were there. If I was shown that poem by a seven year old, I'd say stick to your night-time job, not your day job—keep your night job, the day can look after itself.

I remember one day when I was a kid and sick at home, I had a book of poems somebody had given me and in it was a poem of Shakespeare's, 'Blow blow thou winter wind, thou art not so unkind'. I copied the poem out just to get the feeling of writing a poem down—writing the verse forms and quite deliberately copying it out.

Things changed pretty dramatically when I was sent off in Form One to St Peter's College. I loathed secondary school—I don't have many happy memories of that place. I loathed the narrowness of it all. There was a lot of unhappiness within the school, a fair amount of violence and a lot of frustration. When I look back on certain teachers, all I can think of is incredibly frustrated men wearing these big skirts, big long black skirts—a pretty strange life really.

Brother Lynch

Old Boys – the boys you knew in shorts and
socks, the boys like me – they come to
visit regularly.

Just as I did yesterday, brought
two bottles from
my motel fridge, imagining that three
or a half-dozen would seem
I'd come – not to talk
and talk to you alone, old Lynch –
but come simply
to hit the piss.

I'd never seen you out of uniform,
a chalky black soutane,
a white coat in the science lab.

You wore a green shirt yesterday,
a man at home.
Your old eyes shone.

Of course your Old Boys call
with conversation pieces like
'Do you remember Grant Malloy?'
or 'What of Kevin Mahon?'

– What else (your words), 'in every
man there is the boy,
in every boy the man.'

No, in green shirt yesterday
and me a travel-weary happy man,
we spoke of other things, of
the marriages void of love,
the evening sunlight in the trees,
the winter seamists rolling in.

This was so unlike the school
a thousand miles north you
taught me in – 'They
move us oldies on!'

No seamists there – no sea –
and I never hung round
past four o'clock to watch
the evening in a tree.

But do so now –

and see myself, kept in late,
detention yet again,
heading for the schoolgate –
the boy inside the man,
a thousand poems to write –

the amputated plane trees,
the empty tennis courts,
the grassy bank above where
we smoked our cigarettes –

and in the distance, out of
uniform, the Brothers,
mowing lawns or walking,
solitary men, no
women waiting them.

I leave you, Brother Lynch,
bifocalled bright-eyed man;
can only wish that others
see you as I do –
nothing celibate and sorry,
nothing sad about you.

Meantime, warm cheers, cold beers,
good Brother Lynch,
you have your Heaven yet –
green shirt open to the neck –
an old man
blinking at the sunset.

Sam Hunt, early 1960s

With a love for poems also came what could be described as a rebellion against the strictures of school—short back and sides and all that. While the beauty of the poems was knocking me sideways, high school for me was a bloody nightmare. There were a few good Christian brothers dotted around but you had to look for them—a few kauri among the gorse. When I'd complain about it my mother used to say, 'It'll give you something to react against' or something, and I thought well that's very helpful, I don't want this.

Ken Arvidson was an English teacher at St Peter's who was a great influence. He was a lay teacher who came in part-time; he was also tutoring at Auckland University and became an associate professor of English at Waikato. Ken was a lifesaver for me. If he hadn't come to school, I don't think I would have lasted as long as I did, and I'd just turned sixteen when I left. He introduced me to poets like Gordon Challis, who I've gone on loving ever since.

When I was growing up, you weren't really expected to be thinking about poems, and this is where I'm so grateful to my parents, because they never really contested it. I'd take days off school—and they knew I wasn't at school—and go out to places like Long Bay or Rangitoto Island. The reason for being there was to feel like a poet. It's almost like you had to do your benediction. It was like the novice boy had to put his hours in, he had to stay on a rocky shoreline. I remember, for example, one time on a weekend I got the boat over to Rangitoto Island, around to Drunken Bay (Islington Bay is its official name, but Drunken Bay is its more correct name). In fact, my first poems ever published were called *Rangitoto Cycle* and one of them was called 'Drunken Bay'.

With my sack on my back, I walked over the causeway to Motutapu Island and along the coastline, and stayed out there for about three days, just on my own. The two books I had with me were Ezra Pound's *Selected Poems,* which was bloody good company—quite bizarre company—and Matthew Arnold's *Selected Poems.* I had my writing book and I wrote and wrote. Fortunately the weather was good. When it was time to go back to the mainland on the Sunday I missed the boat—on purpose. I knew there was a phone box at the Drunken Bay store, so I was able to go to the phone box—had my tuppeny piece or whatever—and rang home to let my parents know that the next boat wasn't until Wednesday but I was perfectly safe. I remember my parents should have been much more concerned than they were. I always think they had some sort of belief in me, which continues through to me and my sons—my two boys—my total belief in them.

So I had this vision of somehow living as a poet—that was the lifestyle I envisaged. There were certain New Zealand poets—and other poets from other parts also—who, in a romantic way perhaps, I loved and admired. Poets like Baxter and Alistair Campbell. I was very aware of their presence—they travelled with me. I never sat down thinking, 'I'm now studying New Zealand poetry,' but there were a lot of poems that happened to come from New Zealand. I remember hearing a session on the radio—I would have been twelve years old—on the Concert Programme. There was a monthly programme called 'Poetry', edited by different people. Peter Bland did it very well for a number of years; Louis Johnson hosted it in earlier days. One particular talk was about Alistair Campbell's new book of poems (this was a long time before I knew Alistair), and I think this was my first awareness of him. His poem was read by an actor, and the image came up of the sea. It was a romantic poem suggesting a death—a drowning—and it used the phrase 'the sea, like an unpeopled mirror'. That phrase 'unpeopled mirror' just got to me and that was the moment I first turned on to Alistair's poems.

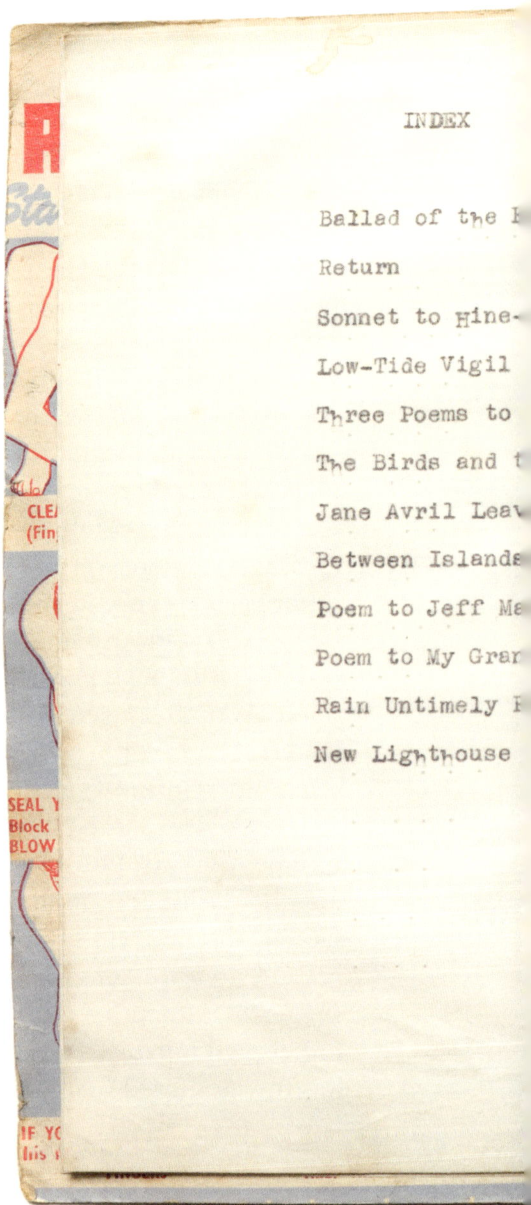

Sam holding a copy of
Between Islands

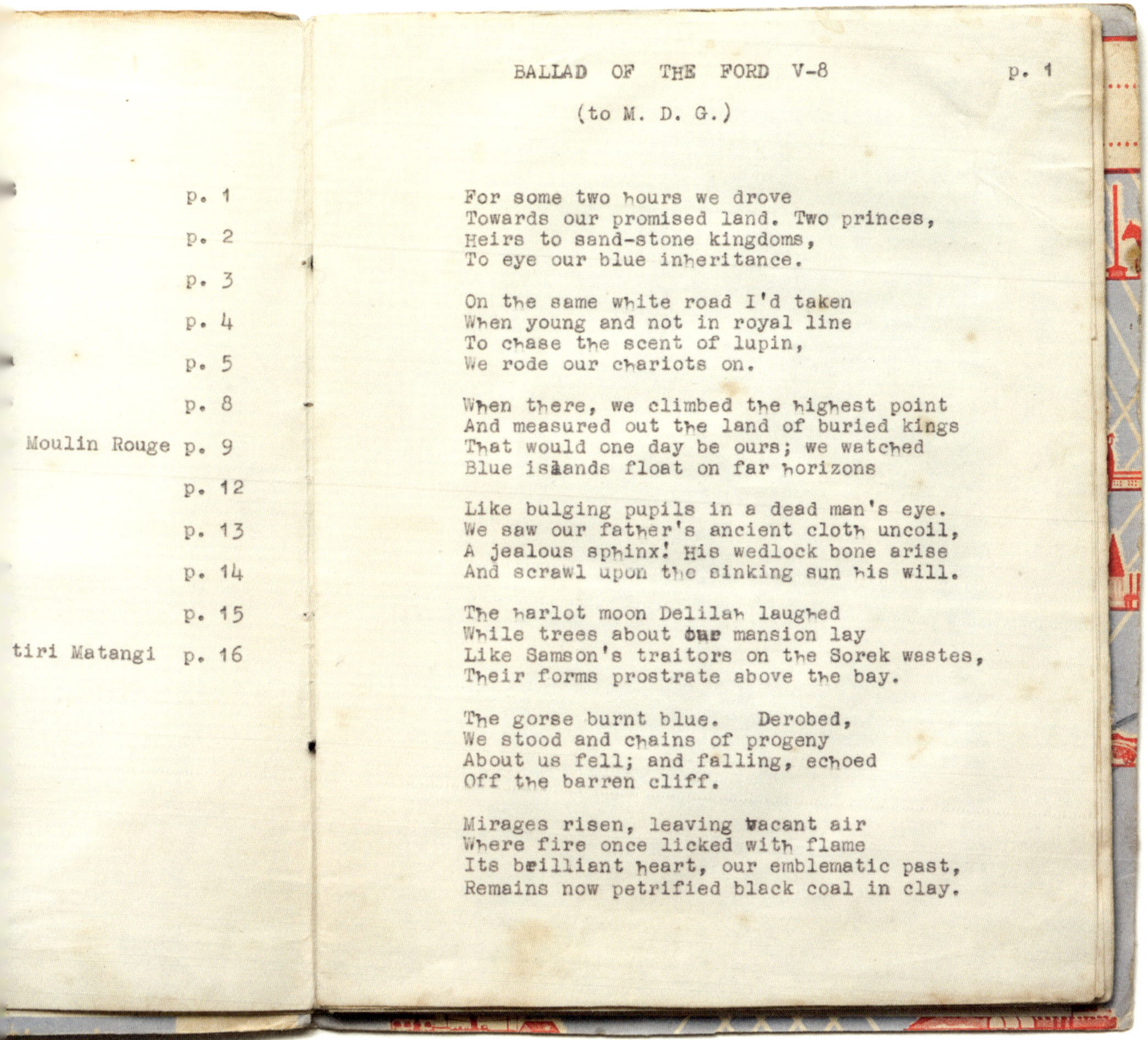

BALLAD OF THE FORD V-8 p. 1

(to M. D. G.)

For some two hours we drove
Towards our promised land. Two princes,
Heirs to sand-stone kingdoms,
To eye our blue inheritance.

On the same white road I'd taken
When young and not in royal line
To chase the scent of lupin,
We rode our chariots on.

When there, we climbed the highest point
And measured out the land of buried kings
That would one day be ours; we watched
Blue islands float on far horizons

Like bulging pupils in a dead man's eye.
We saw our father's ancient cloth uncoil,
A jealous sphinx! His wedlock bone arise
And scrawl upon the sinking sun his will.

The harlot moon Delilah laughed
While trees about our mansion lay
Like Samson's traitors on the Sorek wastes,
Their forms prostrate above the bay.

The gorse burnt blue. Derobed,
We stood and chains of progeny
About us fell; and falling, echoed
Off the barren cliff.

Mirages risen, leaving vacant air
Where fire once licked with flame
Its brilliant heart, our emblematic past,
Remains now petrified black coal in clay.

Sam Hunt's first book of poems, Between Islands, *was self-published when he was sixteen. He hand-typed and bound four copies.*

Betty Hunt

No Bells

(in memory, Betty Hunt)

1

What's it like?
I've seen you, mother, do
what until last Wednesday
neither had dared to.

What's it like,
did it all go dark and
that was that? Or was it all light;
and you, on this occasion, right?

2

Angels are thick on the ground,
toi-toi in full bloom
down the backbone of the land:
as if our time has come –

an end to hate, to lies;
when all things change as if to say
if the angels come this close
God can't be too far away.

3

The bamboo windbells
broke the night you died.

They were there
out on the wide verandah
doing their thing, like wind bells do,
sounding like the last of the laughter
on an Autumn evening;
the next morning, scattered,
four lengths of bamboo, empty shells.

I won't be putting them back up
out on the wide verandah,
not in a hurry.

The wind can blow
hard as it does on the Kaipara.

There'll be no bells.

living the poet's life

I was sixteen when I left school. I sat University Entrance then I left school. By the time I was eighteen I was living in the North, in Kaeo. I got my heavy truck and trailer licence on my eighteenth birthday, the fourth of July, 1964—did that in Kaikohe and that automatically gave me my car licence. I was working at the Moerewa meatworks, and I'd go and put in three solid weeks there and make quite good money. Once there was a bit of a drop-off I could sign off and disappear for a month. Sometimes I'd run out of money but I was quite lucky.

At one stage I was driving trucks in the North, living in a boatshed on the Whangaroa Harbour with a very beautiful Maori girl, Martha. It was a very cushy job driving this old, old truck and trailer. My main runs were from the Bay of Islands through to Awanui, which was a port just north of Kaitaia. I was doing all these things so I could, romantically speaking, live what I imagined was the life a poet would live. I didn't want to be a poet who was actually a civil servant by day. I was aware of the idea that you live one life and you write, and your writing life is more like a secret life, but that never felt like the way I was going to do things. I was always aware of making time to write poems—that I'd live my life in a way that made it possible to listen to the poems.

I did have a couple of short stints at university in these early years, first at Auckland and then at Victoria. Both were very short-lived affairs, I think mostly to appease the parents. At university they were studying people like Browning and other poets I couldn't get into. So it wasn't really for me, and I think instinct in a way told me to stay away from there. It was like you're mistaking your tabernacles, you're getting the wrong tabernacle here. This is a tabernacle of higher learning but hybrid poetry isn't necessarily higher learning. Poetry can come from anywhere, from any level of consciousness, and I think the greatest poems by people have often seemingly come out of nowhere.

I don't know if you've ever seen Jon Stallworthy's book *Between the Lines*, a

Up Moonshine Valley, 1970

study of W. B. Yeats's manuscripts. Stallworthy's approach, even though he was an academic, wasn't so much a study in what was being said, but rather how it was being said. I wouldn't be so inclined to have read, for example, a study on the imagery of Yeats in his later poems—that doesn't interest me—I generally don't find academic approaches to poetry of any help. I think they are talking about poetry, not about poems and there is a very big difference for me. It is a little bit like looking at a motor manual where you get an exploded view—Stallworthy's book is like an exploded view, it's three dimensional, and looking at how Yeats made his poems was great, very interesting.

To see a poem like 'Sailing to Byzantium' and to see where it started and where it finished is amazing. You can't say that Yeats knew where he was going with that one, but he knew when he got there—he'd taken us there, he'd created the place:

> Or set upon a golden bough to sing
> To lords and ladies of Byzantium
> Of what is past, or passing, or to come.

Yeats spent a lot of his time as a young man travelling around Ireland collecting folk tunes. A lot of his early poems came from that whole tradition and I think people forget that. They get hold of a poem from Yeats and analyse it to death, before the poem's had a chance to have a say. For me, if I was going teach a poet's work, someone I liked enough to be teaching—say Yeats or Pablo Neruda or Octavio Paz or Sylvia Plath—I'd make sure the students listened to the poet first and got to know the poet's voice. If the reader has learned, so to speak, how to read the music, he can actually get something off the page.

Sam Hunt, teacher, Mana College, 1967

During these early years I was writing poems but I wasn't out there doing much publicly. Then in 1967 I moved south to Bottle Creek and I got a job teaching, just for twelve weeks as a relieving English teacher at Mana College. I was basically babysitting the kids, but I was also telling them poems. Other teachers at the school would say to me, 'Could you come and look after my class—could you come and give my kids a session?' And so I did, and that's where it started. These sessions turned into sort of shows because my kids—who were low-stream third and fourth form—by the end they knew poems like Sylvia Plath's 'Daddy' off by heart. Years later one of the girls from that class—she's a senior policewoman now—came up to me at an airport and said, 'I still know that poem of Sylvia Plath's.' She quoted me the lines at the airport:

> Every woman adores a Fascist,
> The boot in the face, the brute
> Brute heart of a brute like you.

I had a really bad stutter as an adolescent, and any thought of going on stage was prohibitive. At one stage I thought I'd follow my father's footsteps and become a barrister but I got scared off the idea because I'd be stuttering in court. So I thought I'd become a journalist like my grandfather, maybe. I didn't know what I was going to do and so I did a little bit of teaching and then for the next three years went to teachers' college, in 1968, 1969 and 1970.

A School Report

Working with these young kids in the pastel
clay frontier, we live near bulldozer blades.
The school I came to yesterday had loads
of children waiting: that was all.
The road up the valley still a shingle path.
The town planners never predicted such birth.

They write short poems, the kids. 'I wish I was rich I
wish I had gold wings I am made out of sky…'
They paint houses pastel, and the houses
smudge. I told them this morning how wild horses
and moonshiners lived here once. Late on today
a group of them made a model city of clay.

I trained as a primary teacher at Wellington Teachers' College, and it was a wonderful three years they gave me. I knew I'd never go teaching but you got a salary in those days, $50 a week—bloody marvellous. When I'd gone to my interview for training college in late '67—not long after moving to Bottle Creek—I'd said that I was not convinced that there was any relationship between teaching as it was practised and education in the real sense, but if I were accepted for teachers' college and was convinced after three years of training that such a relationship could exist, I'd be very happy to go teaching—and they accepted me on those terms.

In the last year and a half of those three years I was pretty much my own boss, thanks to a man called Keith Fox, who was the deputy principal of the College. I was writing my poems and had published a few books by this stage, and Keith used to argue that a lot of my assignments were covered by the fact that I was writing poems. So I'd have days off—I had very gentlemanly hours—and every so often during that time I'd be sent out with fellow students on section to work in different schools.

After I finished at teachers' college, I taught for a while in Porirua East, at a school called Maraearoa, where I worked with kids who'd often just come straight from Niue and Tokelau. I loved working with the kids. I didn't have a class, but I was specialising in language, and it was working very well—I had done a lot of it while on section.

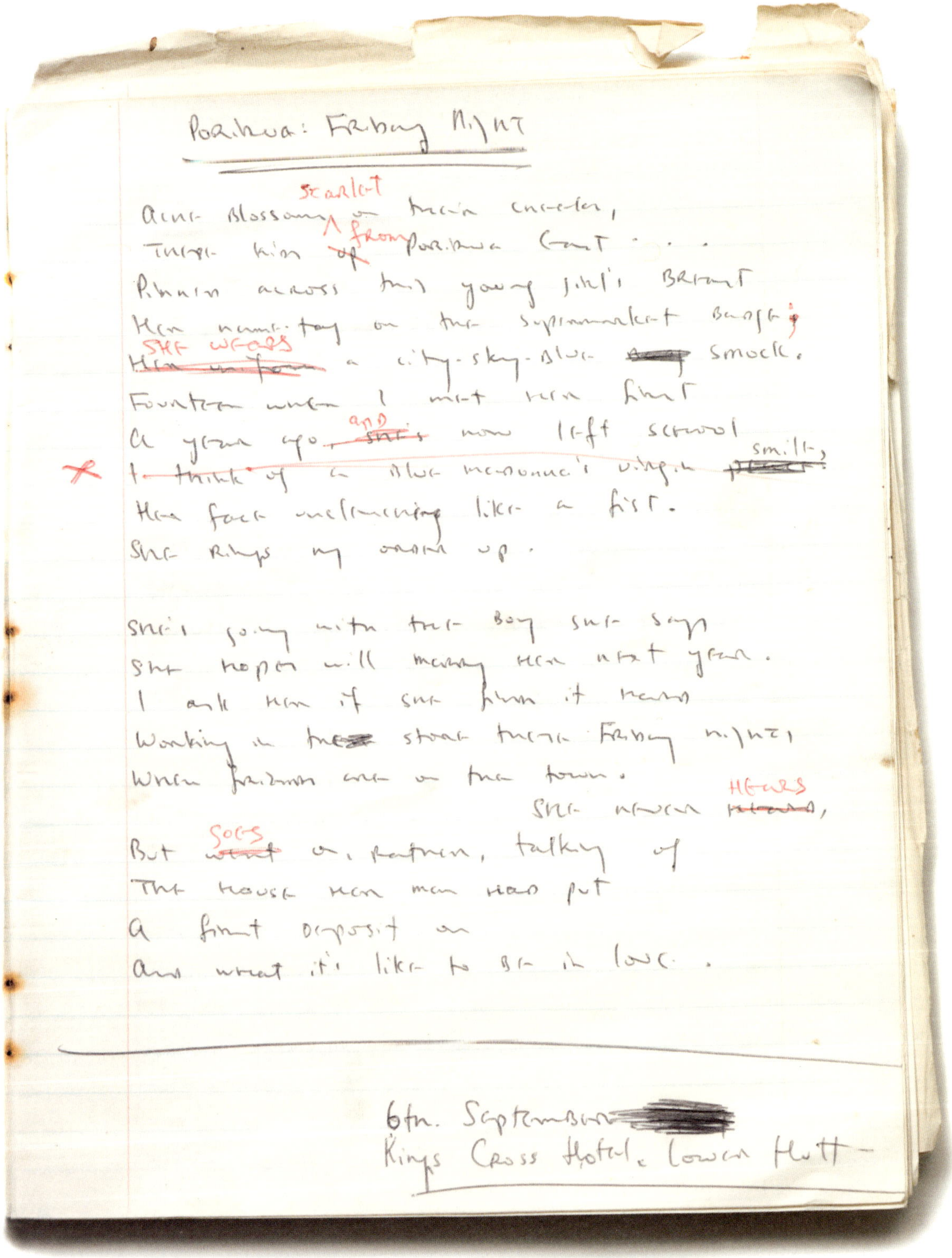

Draft of 'Porirua Friday Night', 1969

Porirua Friday Night

Acne blossoms scarlet on their cheeks,
These kids up Porirua East…
Pinned across this young girl's breast
A name-tag on the supermarket badge;
A city-sky-blue smock.
Her face unclenches like a fist.

Fourteen when I met her first
A year ago, she's now left school,
Going with the boy
She hopes will marry her next year.
I asked if she found it hard
Working in the store these Friday nights
When friends are on the town.

        She never heard:
But went on, rather, talking of
The house her man had put
A first deposit on
And what it's like to be in love.

I always knew I was never going to go teaching when the three years were up. My heart wasn't in it, so I went to see my headmaster, who was very supportive of me—his name was Ron Grey. I said, 'I really am very grateful for everything you've done creating a position for me in the school but it's not what I'm going to do.' I remember feeling bad about it but knowing it was inevitable—and he knew that too. I went up to school that day and said goodbye to my kids, some of whom are still friends. I got to know some great families—I'm still very close to one lovely family from those school days, the Lukatau family from Tokelau.

So then there was the problem of paying back the bond. It wasn't the full amount we were given; it was only $200 each year. So for the three years I owed the education board $600, which, in the early 1970s, was a lot of money—more than I could dream of having to give to anyone. So started an ongoing battle with the Wellington Education Board.

There were different ways you could get out of your bond, including being pregnant or insane. At one stage the letters from the Education Board were getting really heavy. One day I had an important meeting that had been set up by them for me to attend. They didn't see if I could make it—I was simply told to be at an address in Wellington at a certain time. At that time my then girlfriend was heading north to Auckland. She was lovely, a very beautiful girl, Yvette. She said, 'Come up north with me.' So we got up to Mangaweka—this was before I bought the place at Mangaweka, and before my connection with the place was established. We'd stopped at the pub for a few jugs and a game of pool. In those days there was a post office across the road, like the rest of New Zealand small towns.

> A blue flag floats.
> I bought a hot meat pie at the store,
> a new harmonica.

I suddenly remembered I was meant to be at the meeting, so we went across to the post office and I sent the secretary of the Education Board a telegram saying, 'Dear Ivan. Sorry can't make the appointment. Family matters have taken me north. Love and Happy Christmas, Sam Hunt.' I gave the lady behind the desk the telegram. She said, 'Do you want this to go normal rates?' I said it should go urgent because I wanted it to get there as quickly as possible. I was concerned they'd be sitting around waiting for me. It was December, Christmas was coming up, and you could see ads about Christmas telegrams, so I said, 'Make it a Christmas greeting one as well.' Then I thought, how am I going to pay for this? So I said, 'Could you make it collect as well?' So they did. And apparently the place just cracked up laughing—that's what I heard years later.

I remember one time when there was a poetry reading at the teachers' college on a Friday—they used to have the assembly on a Friday and all the students would gather. On this occasion the readers were James K. Baxter, Alistair Campbell, Louis Johnson and myself. Keith Fox chaired it and he introduced each poet in turn. When he came to introduce me, as a fellow student, he said to the audience, 'I don't have to introduce Sam because he's one of our students, but I'll take the opportunity to say that an institution like the Wellington Teachers' College here isn't responsible for just producing teachers. All the people on the stage are poets, as is Sam, and they've all been students at this institution, although none of them is teaching now. If Sam never spends a day teaching in years to come it won't be our loss, it won't be anyone's loss, because he'll make up for it in other ways.'

The year following my urgent Christmas greeting telegram to the Education Board, Keith Fox was talking to one of his friends who was head of English at the teachers' college, Pat Macaskill. Pat was one of the people on the interviewing board when I went for my entrance interview and said I didn't believe there was a connection between teaching as practised and education in the real sense, and so on. Pat told Keith about this, and they found all the notes from the interview. Keith got hold of me with the news, 'You're free of the bond.' He said, 'That day you went for your interview, you'd already established the exit.' So I sent a little note to the secretary thanking him for the three years I had at teachers' college, but saying that 'I wasn't convinced that such a relationship did exist, yours Sam Hunt.' I was out! I didn't have to get pregnant or go mad after all.

In that first year of fulfilling that bond—about April of '71—I'd gone up to Masterton and done a wild show with Mammal in the town hall there. I was doing poems between the bands and doing some stuff with Mammal, and we'd had a full house. I did the show, and I remember the next day walking round the estuary to catch the train to school and working out that I earned more that night than I'd earn in two weeks of school teaching each day.

Sam Hunt, 1966

Until 1971 it hadn't occurred to me to jump—to take the leap into performing. Maybe I was being the middle class boy, not prepared to jump until I knew it was safe. The first show I ever did was in Murrays Bay on the North Shore in Auckland. It was a group called something like the North Shore Players and they had a place out in Murrays Bay called the Outram Hall. The other claim to fame of the Outram Hall—apart from it being my first venue—was that it was once voted the ugliest building in New Zealand, so I knew it was a good place to start. That was my first paid gig and I wasn't long out of school—I would have been about seventeen or eighteen. A member of that group, Peggy Nicholson, was a friend of my mother's and she really got me my first gig. I don't know how much they paid me but they paid me, and I did a good show of all that I'd written at that stage, including 'A Purple Balloon', which I'd just finished.

I've always believed in the telling rather than the reading of a poem. I prefer the word 'told' rather than the word 'read'—there's a big difference. In a funny way, it's a nod to the fact that a Queen's or King's Counsel had a special waistcoat without pockets so that they could not carry notes; while the everyday barrister or lawyer, they would use notes in court. I don't know if this still applies, but I feel a bit like that when I'm doing a show. I don't really want to be getting bits of paper out, and if it's not important enough for me to know by heart, it's not important enough to lay on other people.

When I've had pressure put on me to publish a poem on the page, I've often argued that it's not really where the poem came from, or was aimed at. The page is a way of scoring it. That goes back to the fact that, for me, the world of poems is very much a spoken one. Even within one's head—hearing the words—you're sounding the notes out. Imagine looking at a score of sheet music and reading the notes without actually listening to the notes in your head—that would defeat the point. For me it's exactly the same with poems. I remember as a kid going to Milford, then just a little village on the North Shore of Auckland—in those days there used to be an expression 'Are you married or do you live in Milford?'—it was a de facto sort of place—and there was a little library there with a sign up saying, 'No reading aloud'. I was quite young then and thought, 'How do you read and not read aloud?'

From an early age I had a strong preference for poets doing their own stuff, rather than actors doing it. I remember we had a reading of Dylan Thomas by Richard Burton, who had a beautiful voice. But it's a little bit like people doing versions of Bob Dylan—in the end it's always better to hear the poet telling it. As somebody said, 'the poet's voice is a key to their work.' Now it's not always going to be true. Some poets touch the outer stratosphere and beyond but would bring it down to earth very fast if they started speaking it. Often poets can murder their own stuff—I'm aware of that. Alistair Te Ariki Campbell murdered his stuff on stage yet he had the perfect ear—the words and the score he created are absolutely perfect.

Poets who sing their song with clarity and precision—I would put Pablo Neruda there, Bob Dylan, W. B. Yeats. Not a lot exists of Yeats's reading. He died in 1939, and in 1936 they finally got him into a studio—he was very suspicious of a microphone. As an old man he only recorded poems he wrote as a young man, which is a hell of a shame. I'd love to hear him do some of those later poems.

Hearing poems—that, to me, is the key to it. Having it happen as it was meant to happen—to be heard. Music is written to be heard, and poetry—if it's any good—is music, as far as I'm concerned. If anyone came and showed me a page of musical notes, I'd say, 'Well I'd like to hear it, if you don't mind.' Same thing with a poem; I always like to hear a poem, even if it's inside your own head. You're not always in a position to be reading a poem out loud, but at least you can hear it in your own head.

People sometimes become so immersed in the score—the written version of it—that they miss the real thing. The real thing exists out there with the gods, on the top of the steeple of the church or deep in the cave. Baxter says it all:

Inscription

Within that land there is a range
And on that range there is a cone,
And on that cone there is a rock,
And in that rock there is a cave,
And in that cave there is a stone,
And on that stone I carved a name,

And the cut letters will remain
At length when there are no more men
But only a little dust fallen
On gully, rock and cone.

[James K. Baxter]

There's the idea that the students have got to understand the poem, and to understand the poem, presumably, you've got to dissect it on the page. I'm not against working out why a poem moves you so, or doesn't move you so—that's quite valid I reckon—but to give it a fair go, you've got to hear it. The poem is not just there on the page—it works the whole room, it works the whole space you're in. Many a poem has died a death, crucified, if you like, on the page, when in fact all it wanted—to use the Christian analogy—was a bit of resurrection. I know well how many poems I've fallen in love with but I surely haven't understood them—like certain people I've fallen in love with but have never understood.

Here's an example of falling in love with something you don't understand. My parents had a friend whose name was Nora. She came from Hungary. All her brothers had been shot in front of her but somehow, miraculously, she survived and got out of Hungary. By the time she made New Zealand, one of her great heroes, József Attila—a poet, he was thirty-two years old—had died. She used to say—in the company of me (I was ten years old) and my mum and dad, and usually a few other people—she used to say this poem in Hungarian, and I can still now, at the age of sixty-two, hear the sound of that poem very clearly in my head. I can't speak Hungarian but I was besotted, totally and utterly besotted by that poem. I used to say to Nora when she came over, 'Nora, can you do the poem, the József Attila?' and she'd say, 'When we've had a few drinks, Sam.' The poem's a mindblower, even in translation:

The Seventh

If you set out in this world,
better be born seven times.
Once, in a house on fire,
once, in a freezing flood,
once, in a wild madhouse,
once, in a field of ripe wheat,
once, in an empty cloister,
and once among pigs in sty.
Six babes crying, not enough:
you yourself must be the seventh.

When you must fight to survive,
let your enemy see seven.
One, away from work on Sunday,
one, starting his work on Monday,
one, who teaches without payment,
one, who learned to swim by drowning,
one, who is the seed of a forest,
and one, whom wild forefathers protect,
but all their tricks are not enough:
you yourself must be the seventh.

If you want to find a woman,
let seven men go for her.
One, who gives heart for words,
one, who takes care of himself,
one, who claims to be a dreamer,
one, who through her skirt can feel her,
one, who knows the hooks and snaps,
one, who steps upon her scarf:
let them buzz like flies around her.
You yourself must be the seventh.

If you write and can afford it,
let seven men write your poem.
One, who builds a marble village,
one, who was born in his sleep,
one, who charts the sky and knows it,
one, whom words call by his name,
one, who perfected his soul,
one, who dissects living rats.
Two are brave and four are wise;
You yourself must be the seventh.

And if all went as was written,
you will die for seven men.
One, who is rocked and suckled,
one, who grabs a hard young breast,
one, who throws down empty dishes,
one, who helps the poor win;
one, who worked till he goes to pieces,
one, who just stares at the moon.
The world will be your tombstone:
you yourself must be the seventh.

[József Attila]

At the same time—certainly with me growing up with a lot of great books, beautiful books, great volumes of poems—the image of the words on the page was deeply impressed on me. The score and the rendition of it are almost inseparable. David Eggleton said, in a review of the *Doubtless* poems, that there's a certain 'richness' to be gotten from the page which doesn't necessarily come over from the stage. And that's dead true.

I used to think when I first set out on the road doing lots of shows that the public side could burn out the private lamp—and I think at times it did. I think one of the dangers of becoming recognised in a small community like New Zealand is that you can start believing the stuff they write about you, especially if they are writing nice or interesting things. For a certain length of time, I hope not long, this happened to me, and it can be quite a negative force. But if in fact you can get smart about it—and it took me quite a few years—you can actually make one work off the other rather than countering the other, as there is a lot of dramatic energy out there, power to be harnessed. I always think of that beautiful line from Bob Dylan's 'Dark Eyes'—'A million faces at my feet and all I see are dark eyes'—a wonderful, magical, mystical line. I think he is making the point that despite the thousands, or in his case millions of people, he is actually just seeing one pair of dark eyes. And that's where you need to aim the poem. If you can get to that person, you can get to the rest of them, but you always need some heart to aim at.

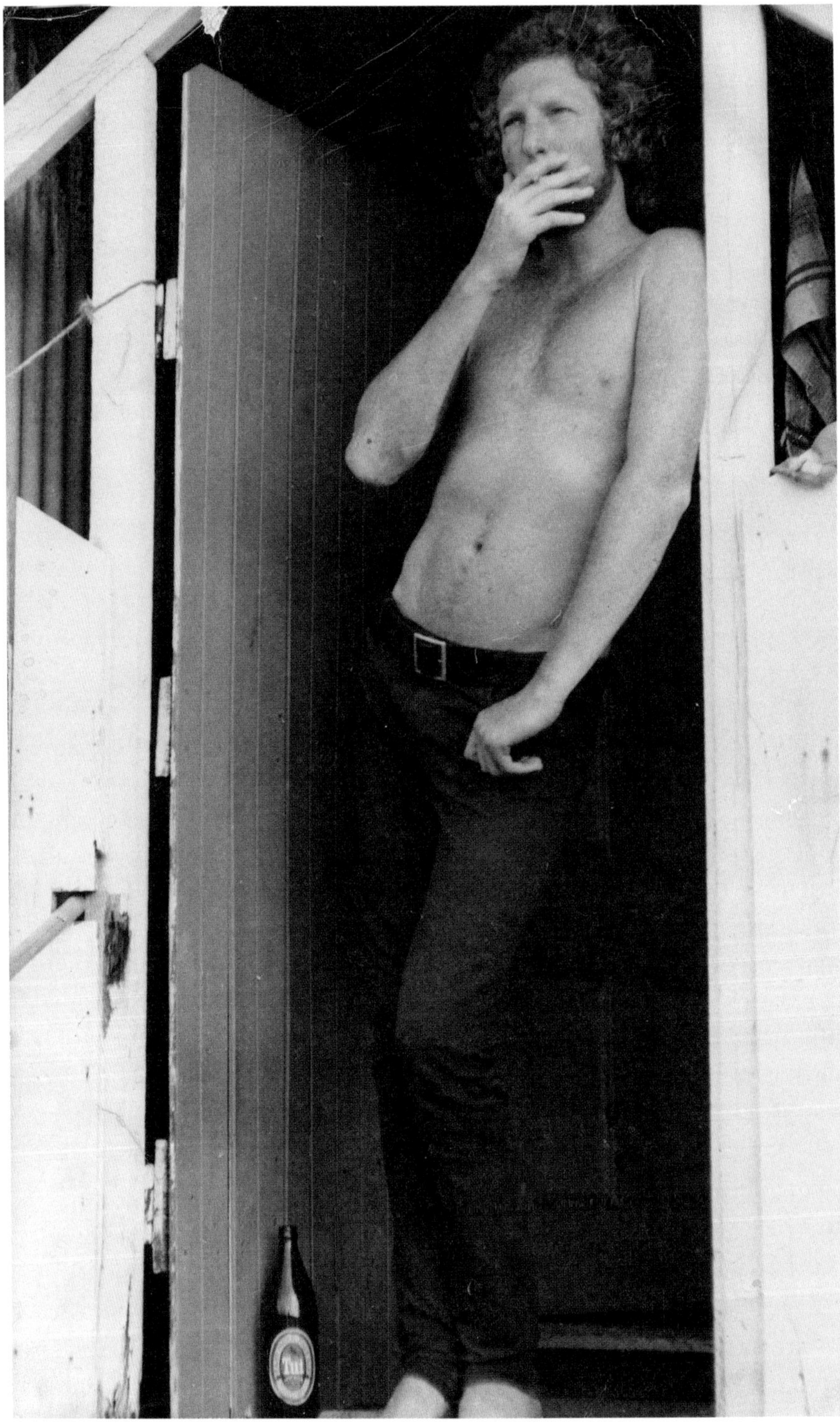

Outside one of the Bottle Creek baches, 1971

New Words

New words, the words I have not
told, they gather for the night.

I send them out each day, each
tolling on its own. They reach

I know not where. They bounce back
reeling, some ready to break,

some merely echoing. They
bring back their news of the day

told in each one's way. They come
back tired, relieved to be home.

These words, the words I have not
told, they settle for the night.

Then, and only then, I light
the lamp, work on them, work late;

coax and grill. Interrogation
does not let up till the dawn.

Some nights, a few surrender,
tell me all I need know—her

dreams, the rhythms of her heart.
That's when there's a poem in it.

When I was in my twenties there were old literary people who disapproved of what I was doing, they disapproved strongly and were highly suspicious of my taking poems into pubs and jails and other lock-ups, parliament and other hang-outs. There was the odd person in the literary world who said to me, 'This will be your death as a poet, as a lyric poet, becoming public property.' Maybe there was a time when the lamp was blown out—maybe it had quite a bit to do with that dryness of mind I've talked about—that unproductive decade starting in the 1990s. Maybe part of it was a process of levelling it all out, getting to the point where you can feed the lamp, if you like, with the oil and sweat of the public shows. Certainly one way the performing of poems can feed the creating of poems is that if you're doing them live every night and you're listening to your poems all the time, you start to know what works. I know any number of people who have said this in different ways—from Leonard Cohen to my friend Barry Saunders and others. There's some line that you're almost feeling embarrassed about, and later you think, 'Why was I embarrassed by that line? What's wrong with it?' and quite often by the next time you do it live, you've already struck the line out.

Performing is an extraordinary process of feedback, which the vast majority of poets would never have, and possibly would not know how to handle. I'm not suggesting I always handle it perfectly today, but I am suggesting that maybe I'm more able to work it in my favour than when I was a young man. You know when you're a young man and you get your photo in the paper and you're on television and you're voted the most recognisable or whatever, you think, 'I should have been a town clock, I got the wrong job.' So there are distractions and I think anyone who chooses to live a different life has got to learn to live with those things and to make them work for them.

My father used to tell me a poem, a funny old poem of Charles Kingsley's called 'The Three Fishers'—it's a great poem. I was doing a show with the Warratahs and I was doing this poem up on stage. It has three verses and I got to the end of the second verse and couldn't remember the start of the third verse, so I said to the audience, 'Look, excuse me. I seem to have blown this one. It's lost in the ether out there,' and then got on with some others. At half-time I was ringing my son Alf, who was then about five or six. I rang Alf to say goodnight and I said, 'Darling, can you remember that poem "The Three Fishers"? Can you remember how the last verse starts?' He said, 'Three corpses', and I went back on stage in the second half and said, 'Well the lost line has come back, it's all forgiven', so I said the poem:

The Three Fishers

Three fishers went sailing away to the West,
  Away to the West as the sun went down;
Each thought on the woman who lov'd him the best;
  And the children stood watching them out of the town;
For men must work, and women must weep,
And there's little to earn, and many to keep,
    Though the harbour bar be moaning.

Three wives sat up in the lighthouse tower,
  And they trimm'd the lamps as the sun went down;
They look'd at the squall, and they look'd at the shower,
  And the night rack came rolling up ragged and brown.
But men must work, and women must weep,

Though storms be sudden, and waters deep,
   And the harbour bar be moaning.

Three corpses lay out on the shining sands
  In the morning gleam as the tide went down,
And the women are weeping and wringing their hands
  For those who will never come back to the town;
For men must work, and women must weep,
And the sooner it's over, the sooner to sleep;
   And good-bye to the bar and its moaning.

[Charles Kingsley]

Isn't it lovely? My dad told me that poem and then years later I'm doing it in a show and I ring my child at half-time to get him to give me a prompt. I need a prompt now and again. My father would have loved that. He'd have probably put down the loss of memory to overindulgence in certain things, but when you've got a couple of thousand poems up there, this does happen sometimes.

Tour poster, 2000s

SAM HUNT
in concert
BETWEEN ISLANDS TOUR
26th & 27th September
The Troubadour, 388 Brunswick St, Fitzroy
29th September
Greendale Hotel, near Blackwood
1st & 2nd October
Kamikaze Cafe, 210 Toorak Road, South Yarra

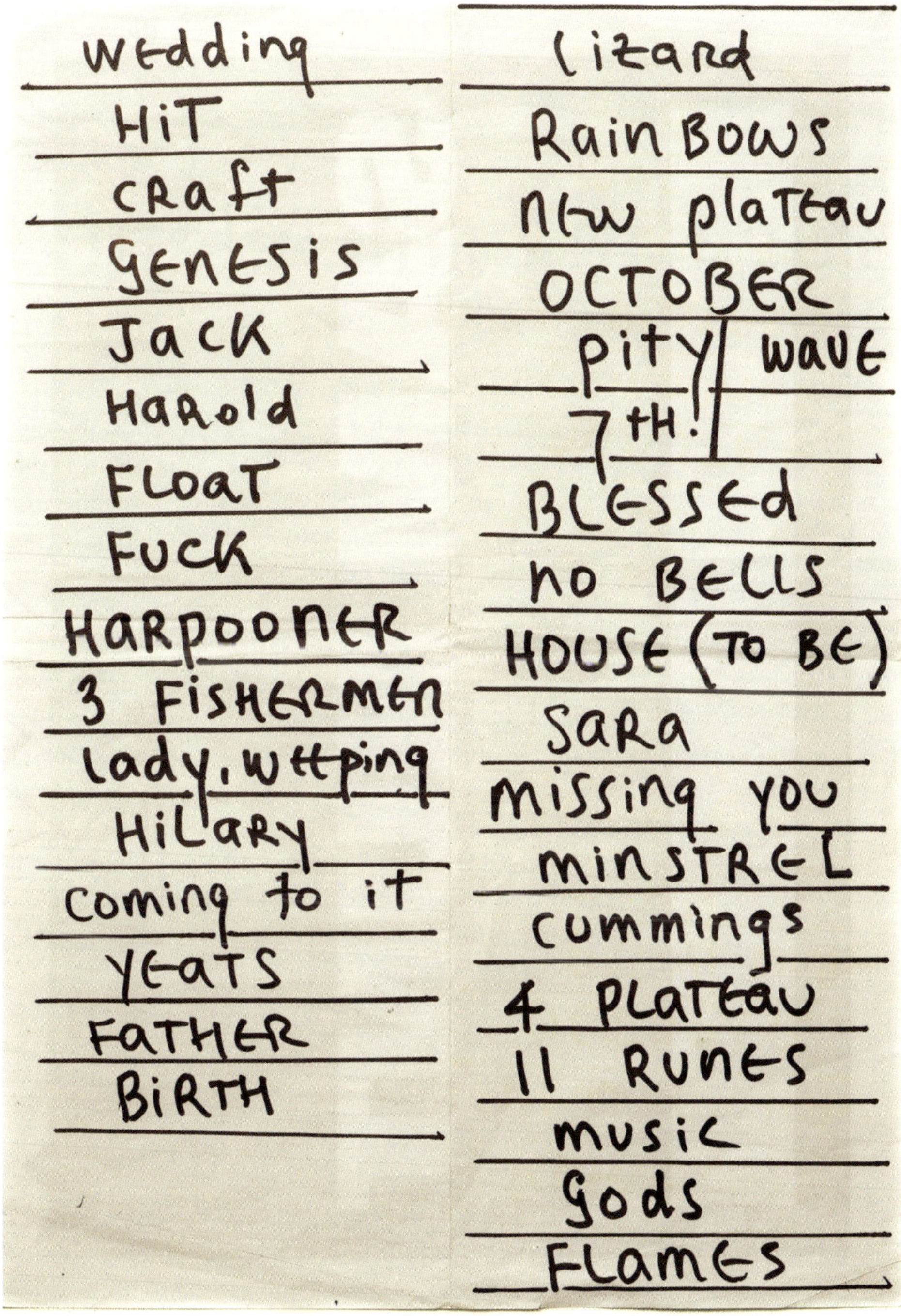

Tour poster and set list

interrogating the silence

Where do poems come from? Dylan Thomas has this great line where he says: 'The best craftsman always leaves holes and gaps in the works of the poem so that something that is not in the poem can creep, crawl, flash, or thunder in.' And then he goes on to quote Yeats, 'Everything happens in a blaze of light'.

Now there are a lot of people around who say inspiration is not a magic notion, that there is no such thing, and that you just need to be at your writing desk at 9 o'clock in the morning. If you're not there, you're not a writer. There's another school, of which I am a member, who would say 'bullshit'. I'm never going to be near a writing desk at 9 o'clock in the morning. I admit that it would be a good thing if I could do that more often—and sometimes I do put disciplines on myself because I know how distracting things can be—but essentially inspiration is ninety per cent of the process in making poems.

My mother told me that from an early age, I always had the feeling that to make poems up one had to go through a cleansing process and that you needed silence. Every poem is a prayer, in a sense. I experienced that silence both in the process of poem making and, being brought up a Catholic, with prayer.

George Mackay Brown's poem 'The Poet' says it all for me. The last lines are:

> His cold stare
> Returned to its true task, the interrogation of silence.

All I can do is concur. I do believe there's a process of clearing out, of finding 'the pool of silence' to make a good poem. And I think it's possibly why people who put themselves in that position of interrogating silence and getting to the position where they can interrogate silence, when you are being eye-balled by God, are in quite a vulnerable state. It's not always like this—sometimes it's more casual and maybe I'm over-emphasising it, but it's always got an element of that to it.

And it's often hard to find silence if you're here, there and everywhere, and people want to talk to you on the radio, and people want this and that. For example, right now I haven't written a poem for weeks because I haven't had the chance to listen for one. But then again, if I was—let's say—a bus driver, I'd be having distractions from my poems too, I'd be having to drive a bus, for a start. Or a university lecturer—that could be even worse. I've seen a lot of people who had the writing bug lose it going to university, often, I think, because they became too self-conscious. One friend of mine, he wrote good poems and then he went to university, did an MA in English and he got scared. He published some beautiful poems as a young man but he said to me, 'You know, in the end I got scared off'; he knew too much about it. To be a publishing poet, for example, in an English Department at a university would be a fairly brave act.

So creating or allowing space for the poem is important to me. Sometimes you may appear semi-reclusive—apart from when you go on stage—but I like that. I like the complete contrast between doing the show, which is sort of public but private, and the silence backstage. By the silence backstage, I don't only mean backstage physically at the venue but the backstage of life—making sure you've got the silences you need.

There are different approaches you can take—you just have to find the ones that work. A few years ago, through a friend of mine, I got interested in the Transcendental Meditation movement. TM was, in its own way, for me, very similar to what I'd been doing. To get to certain poems I often go through a process that I understand to be very close to that of meditation—with one big exception: in my case I have a poem at the end of it.

Other little things often happen that let me know a poem's on its way—like a mother getting labour pains, contractions, breaking the waters, the whole lot! And also twinges of moodiness. Sometimes it's just a seemingly spontaneous action; the poem just seems to happen. There are different sorts of poems, and there are different families of poems, but the poems I like most, the ones I feel happiest with, and the ones I love most when they come from someone else, are instant poems. I recognise them straight away. The pure poem, the pure lyric poem, burns with a white-hot light of its own. It's like an acetylene torch. And I would love to say I've written heaps of them, but actually I've written bugger all. But when it happens, it is lovely to do, a simple little poem that literally comes out of nowhere.

I've talked to a lot of people, such as my friend Alistair Campbell, about this. One of his poems which is in this category is a great love poem, one of the simplest love poems in the language but one of the most powerful, called 'Why Don't You Talk To Me?' I said to Alistair one day years ago, 'Where did you get the last line of that poem?' which is 'Why don't you talk to me?' He said, 'I wrote

Mana boathouse, 1983—renovations followed!

the poem up until the last line but couldn't finish it off, and it sat around for ten years, and one day the phrase "why don't you talk to me?" came into my mind and became the title and the last line.' Suddenly it became a poem, it just took—like building something and putting the final piece in. I knew from his words that this was a totally inspired poem—there's no intellectual process, it's coming out of somewhere else. It's coming out of where things like fire and electricity and women come from.

Why Don't You Talk to Me?

Why do I post my love letters
in a hollow log?
Why put my lips to a knothole in a tree
and whisper your name?

The spiders spread their nets
and catch the sun,
and by my foot in the dry grass
ants rebuild a broken city.
Butterflies pair in the wind,
and the yellow bee,
his holsters packed with bread,
rides the blue air like a drunken cowboy.

More and more I find myself
talking to the sea.
I am alone with my footsteps.
I watch the tide recede
and I am left with miles of shining sand.

Why don't you talk to me?

[Alistair Campbell]

When you're talking about the beginnings of a poem, you're talking about a subconscious act—largely. A lot of consciousness comes into it later but the good poems—the real poems—they come from something beyond us. The subconscious seems to be the powerhouse of the poems—that's why dreams are so important. You know when you come out of a dream—you wake up and you've got other distractions—you can forget your dream. I'm sure everyone's had that experience

The beginning of 'A White Gentian', journal 1969

THE MAN HE HOLDS THE DAY
HE HOLDS A BLUE BALLOON ...
A MOUNTAIN CAME TO ME

I BROUGHT A FLOWER FROM THE MOUNTAIN
I PUT IN A JAR

I BROUGHT A FLOWER DOWN
SMELLING OF THE MOUNTAIN

SOMEONE SAYS IT SMELLS OF SEX
I SAY IT SMELLS OF YOU

... AND IS IT NOT ENOUGH
I BRING A FLOWER DOWN
SMELLING OF THE MOUNTAIN ...?

HANGOVER, SITTING ON THE BALCONY

ABOVE A MOUNTAIN CALLED
I'll call it morning.

[...so let it be enough
I bring white flowers down
smelling of the mountain]

Reconsiliation

You came & hardly spoke;
and then last night, ~~you were~~ wiped out
~~wiped out a whistling song one song;~~
a whistling song ~~for me~~ one song
you ~~can't~~ want remember what
the morning as you ~~did~~ ~~go~~ ~~went~~ go
climbing ~~scrambling into the~~ slopes...
a ~~thousand feet to snow~~;
~~I watched you~~ go;
By noon a thousand feet,
~~your figure~~ coming to the snow;
soon y

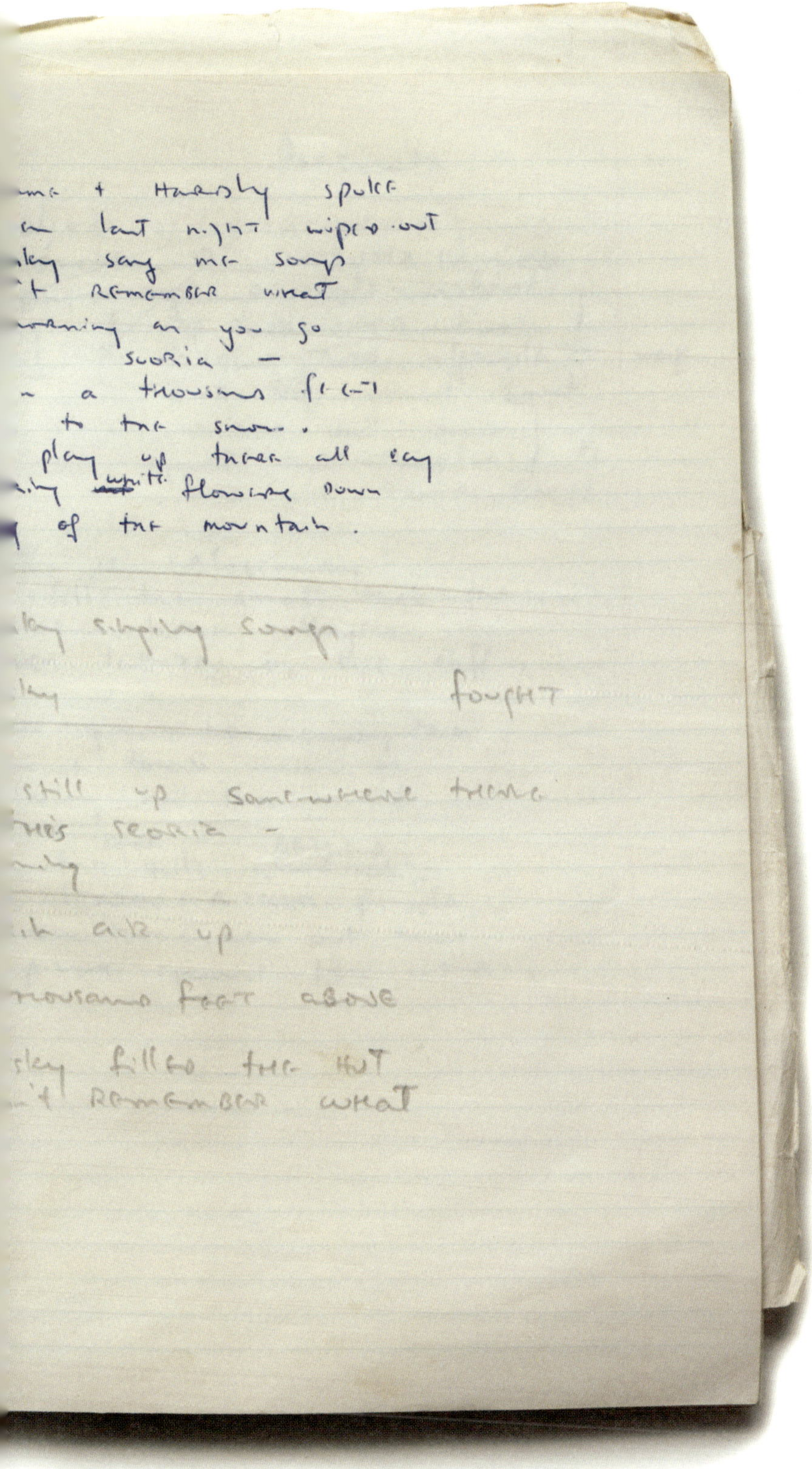

A White Gentian

Remember Ruapehu,
that mountain, six months ago?
You sat in an alpine hut
sketching scoria, red
rusted outcrops in the snow.

I climbed some southern peak
and made up the sort of song
men climbing mountains sing:
how, no longer your lover,
I knew it was over.

I thought I'd try out my song
when I returned that evening
as though there were nothing wrong.
Instead I brought a flower down
smelling of the mountain.

of some elusive dream that you can just get a hold on before it disappears again. Grasping a poem is so much like cracking a dream.

There are ways into the subconscious. One is to have the exercise book and scribble, or a dictaphone, and put the line down straight away, not thinking, 'I'll wait till I wake up tomorrow morning and put the light on,' because sure as hell, there won't be a line to write the next morning because you won't be able to remember it. Years ago I wrote a poem about a girlfriend of mine who was killed in a car smash, a poem called 'Lyn'. It goes, 'I find my poems written down between 2 a.m. in winter and the dawn.' I suppose, looking back on it, I was discovering back then when I wrote those lines, that when you are in that half-conscious state, that's when the lines can come flooding in.

I've always been interested in the Catholic mass and the idea of consecration. I was brought up to believe that the bread actually became the body, and the wine the blood, and as an altar boy I was fascinated by the notion of alchemy, that something could be transformed. Alchemy is one thing though—what most interests me is the process of creation, when you're actually creating something that didn't exist before you came into the room that day or into the world that day. I'm not talking about any old poem, I'm talking about the ones that define your life and maybe help other people define a little bit of their lives.

If I dissect the inspiration—the moment the poem starts to happen in some way that you can recognise, acknowledging also the fact that it's probably been happening a long time before you recognise it—I become aware, particularly so with certain sorts of poems, of a voice. The poem's got its own voice already, and I know the sound of that voice. It's a bit like recognising a voice in a conversation going on in a busy room while you're listening from the outside—suddenly you'll hear a voice of somebody you're close to. That's the poem talking. It may be a voice I've heard before in other poems. You get poems that are from families of poems which are in that particular voice or key, to use that musical term.

I think Beethoven said that he knew what the key of any work was going to be long before he composed it. And I too hear the key, and I think that's right—you hear the key to the voice. It's more than just the tone of voice—there's a sound to it. That's what you lose if you don't have the space. I could possibly have charted out where I wanted the poem to go with a few notes, but even if I had the notes, I think without the voice then I've lost the poem, that's how fragile it is.

The voice or the key or the tone of voice—there's a particular recognisable sound to it. As an example, sometimes I write poems that are quite edgy or nervy, and there's quite a nervy voice in my head. I know those poems when they're going to happen. When you hear the voice, your job is, in some cases, to scribble it down and that's it. At other times, when there's more work involved, that's when you go to the office.

On the road

You think, 'Where does that come from?' Having written a poem which you're pleased with, you can take your head apart to see if it's still ticking or your heart to see if it's still ticking—and try simply to remember the moment when the first pump drove the poem along—like the moment of conception. I can go back to the start of a poem and work back, like remembering a dream. Where did that image come from? Who told you that story? What ferry were you on? Where were you going? It's interesting when someone else comes along later and picks up the evidence—which is the poem, the song, the lyric—and instinctively uncovers the point of conception—often musicians and songwriters, who have practised ears, are good at this.

Once a poem's happening—especially a good one, one that's not forced but helped along, like a midwife delivering a baby—you need to keep on listening, keep tuned in and remembering that that is the way a poem is composed. And it seems logical to me that to take the poem to the next stage, apart from writing it down to remember it, is to tell it, to take it to the public.

And also I've often had poems known and made up, but haven't really known I've made them up, so haven't thought about writing them down. Then I can know the poem and say the poem and I don't even think I've written it down—quite often I haven't done. If I look back in an exercise book I may find some lines written down which ultimately led to the poem that came into my head.

With distractions coming in all the time, it's easy to avoid writing poems. That's why I never allow anyone to pop in. I'm not a popper-in—I don't pop in on people—and I don't want people popping in on me. You've heard about the man from Porlock, the man who interrupted Samuel Taylor Coleridge while he was writing 'Kubla Khan'. The man from Porlock happened to be going by on the highway, on the walkway, and decided to call in on Sam Coleridge, who was, one, on drugs and, two, writing 'Kubla Khan', and he did not want a popper-in from Porlock. His vision was interrupted and he was left with only a fragment of the poem. In every sense one sets out to stop the metaphoric 'popper-in from Porlock' coming and disturbing things.

I've had my man from Porlock—this happened only a few months ago. 'Knock, knock, knock' on the door, and I thought, 'That's unusual'. No one had given me a ring and I did have a poem going on. It was the meter man and he'd got stuck. Well I went out and gave him a hand and hauled him out, and then went back but the poem was gone. That sort of left me feeling like I'd delivered a stillbirth. Something had gone wrong. He meant no harm, but it was a poem I would have liked to have got. I've got it written down in one of the books here, and I suppose I ask myself whether what's gone is the voice of the poem.

I don't know if influence is a word I want to use too strongly around my poems. I know there is such a thing as influence in that you hear something and it's beautiful and it must affect you but it's more subtle than that. I've never deliberately been influenced and I've certainly never consciously decided I wanted to write a poem like that one there by somebody else, it's just never come into the order of things, just like I've never written a poem holding my pen with my foot. It's just one of those things I've never done

I do know about some influence though when it comes to Thom Gunn, that great poet who died a few years ago. He did something pretty unusual among poets of this and last century—he invented his own verse form. People had toyed with it but, as far as I know, he invented the constant use of the seven-syllable line and the particular rhyme schemes or the half-rhyming couplets. I'll give you an example: 'the ice plant is not in **flower**, it extends as springy **floor**'.

Here are classic seven-syllable lines, from 'My Sad Captains':

> One by one they appear in
> the darkness a few friends, and…

He's quite an acquired taste but I love him. Thom Gunn would probably have been the most conscious, the most deliberate influence that I'm aware of. I wouldn't think I was influenced by him in terms of subject matter but certainly in terms of finding structures to help you say what you want to say.

One of the first seven-syllable rhyme poems I wrote when I was very young was 'Flutemaker':

Flutemaker
(a lament)

More regular than clockwork,
the sad retired captain down
the dune path would hobble for
sands where all night oceans break,
and with the sunlight roam,
dazed, the orphanage of the shore.

Poised like day he would then scan
forms abandoned by surf the
night before … gnomons now on
a sun-struck dial of shore;
and like the day, move through the
arc traced out by the flotsam.

Many white years later, late
one evening, the bent captain
found the form he'd searched so long
from which he would carve a flute;
marry his dry silences,
age and frailty, in song.

Up in his shack on the dunes
he chiselled all through the night,
until when day broke he knew
his brittle labour was done:
so the captain pursing tight
dry lips, down the white shaft blew.

And dark, giving itself up
in long slivers to distilled
shrill white shafts of morning sun,
left sunlight dancing on the
bent shadow of a crippled
captain whistling on the dunes.

Quite often, when I'm working on a poem, I'll work on the discipline of giving it a particular syllabic line count to keep the structure and to keep it within, for me, workable bars—a line for me is a bar of music. Often when I've finished a poem I'll throw a hand grenade at it—maybe something a little bit smaller, a double happy or a mighty cannon—and just blow it up. I've needed the set square and the plan to build it—I've needed the discipline to get me there—but once it's built and it exists, I can disguise the discipline.

I'm always interested in verse form but I never let it get in the way of what's happening. For me a perfect poem is when the 'what' of the poem and the 'how' of the poem become inseparable—so you can't say it any other way. It's really what Ezra Pound meant when he said, 'Poetry is a language which cannot be translated.' In its real essence he's right—it exists as it is. When I go to high schools I say to the kids, 'If you get a question in your exam to do with my poems and the examiner asks, "What is the poet saying?" you simply write the whole poem out again, word for word. That's what the poet is saying, and you'd be demonstrating that you understand that in a good poem you cannot divorce what's being said from how it's being said. And if I were marking the exam, I'd give you ten out of ten.'

I remember many years ago I met a girl at Westlake Girls High School who was writing poems. She used a phrase to describe how she felt about poems: she didn't like cutting the wings off butterflies to see how they can fly because they're not going to fly again. She liked to watch to see how they flew but she didn't want to tear the wings off so she could have a closer look. It was actually more important to leave them on. I'm not against analysis of a poem—often it's good. When Bob Dylan or Leonard Cohen bring out a new album you hear the songs for the first time and you may like the tune and you may pick up a few words but beyond that, it's got to have the power to drag you back to listen to it again, and if so that's great. You discover the song or poem as you listen to it.

One of the things that goes with the making up of poems—or the overused words create, creative, the creative light—is that there is always that chance you will come to the edge of that great cliff of silence—in other words, you dry up. When I was young I used to think about it but it never happened to me, because when you're young it's easy—you're saying things for the first time. The young poet has a lot of material—you don't have to dig very deep, perhaps. So when I was young I used to think about what it would be like to dry up.

I was very aware of poets like Allen Curnow—I don't know the background but there seemed to be a pretty big silence there before he kicked into his great poems in his later years. And R. A. K. Mason—he was very good to me. When I knew him he was soon to die and he had, if you like, dried up. He'd written those wonderful poems—gosh, most of his great poems he'd written as a teenager in the 1900s and 1910s—poems like 'Judas Iscariot'—a wonderful poem. But apart from the

Motel, 1980s

odd one during the Korean War—he wrote a great poem 'Sonnet to MacArthur's Eyes'—he wrote no poems in the last thirty years of his life. He talked to me about the poems deserting him—that's the phrase he used. He was a very sombre man then. What he would have been like if he'd still been making the poems up—if the poems had still been coming out and hitting him—I don't know.

The more intensely lyric the poet, I guess, the greater the chances are of that flame dimming. Certainly at periods of your life it's going to happen. Some poets are so uninspired and uninspirational that they keep on writing the same stuff all their life, every day. All they've got to do is sit down and it pours out. There are a lot of poems which are just head exercises, and I'm not talking about those sort of poems or the sort of people who write them. But the lyric poet who does live for Yeats's 'blaze of light' knows that the blaze is not going to take place every day or every week or even every year. The blaze of light could be echoes of darkness, the abyss. Sometimes there's no light there, and I know that as well as anyone. Fairburn, I know, suffered from that. It can be a very depressing thing. You've lost that blaze of light.

In later years I certainly experienced drying up. I consider the period between 1995 and 2005 not actually barren as I was writing poems—making them up, composing them—but basically not liking what I was doing. I showed a friend a few of those poems recently and he said, 'You're being stupid, these are good poems,' so who knows? But there've certainly been times when there've been no poems—good, bad or indifferent—but I've never panicked about it.

One of the first religious poems I became aware of was St Francis of Assisi's ode to the father, son and so on. One of his phrases, which I have always loved, was 'Ask for nothing and refuse nothing.' Although I wasn't a particularly virtuous boy, young chap—I'd get into trouble and things—I had my own virtue and it came from St Francis of Assisi on that particular subject. It made me realise that every poem is a gift. You don't know really where it comes from. Even when I wrote a poem that I may, five minutes later, have torn up and thrown away, or completely dismissed and turned against, nonetheless at the moment of composition it was a gift. One of the other things I was brought up with was reasonably good manners and I was taught not to demand things, so when I did come to the time of drying up over a period of around a year—in about 1995—where I didn't write a single poem, I didn't feel I should demand anything.

It was a really odd experience for a person who had always written poems and always been there to write—I'd just start scribbling and something would happen. But I kept scribbling—I scribbled a lot—maybe longer than a year. I've always had the belief that to write you must write. It may sound like I'm contradicting myself when I'm also talking about the moment it happens, but to make that moment of composition happen you've got to work on it. You can't just wait for the inspiration. You can't just wait for the bolt of lightning from the sky. You have to be in a position that, when inspiration does hit, you're able to cope with it.

I remember years ago I was with Hone Tuwhare—we were doing a show in a Wanganui girls' school—and I remember a pupil putting her hand up and saying to Hone, 'How does a poem happen for you?' He said, 'Well, it's a bit like you go out in that playground there, there's just a chance a seagull could fly over and shit on your shoulder. It's a bit like that. But you've got to get out to the playground so the seagull can get you.' They thought that was great.

A beautiful part about this whole thing is that when the time is over—if you like, your forty days and forty nights in the desert are over, or whatever metaphor you want to use for these things—and the poem comes along, that's a wonderful time. Even if you've had only a few weeks without anything you're happy with and then something happens—it's still wonderful.

The reason I never panicked too much when the dry times came was because I associate poems with pleasure. Poetry wasn't something I had to do or study or anything like that, or write essays on—it was an enjoyable thing. There's a lovely line in the opening poem of Baxter's sequence 'Pig Island Letters', which is dedicated to Maurice Shadbolt: 'Anyone who listens long enough will write again'. It's written in Dunedin, I think from the Otago Peninsula, and that's the sort of landscape of the poem. I don't know whether Maurice Shadbolt was going through a dryness—I imagine he was for Baxter to have written that line. It's got a lot of faith in it. That poem came out when I was a young lad and I remember latching on to that line very mindfully, thinking 'Oh yeah, you've got to do that, you've got to keep scribbling, keep listening.' And faith, to have faith in the silence and also realise the silence is there for a reason—not necessarily a good reason but a reason.

from *Doubtless*

'I like this place'
said the erudite poet
as he stepped up my stairs,
'I like it a lot!'

I told him, 'Fuck you, poet,
this place is my house.'
And I kicked him down the stairs.
With all my heart. With all of it.

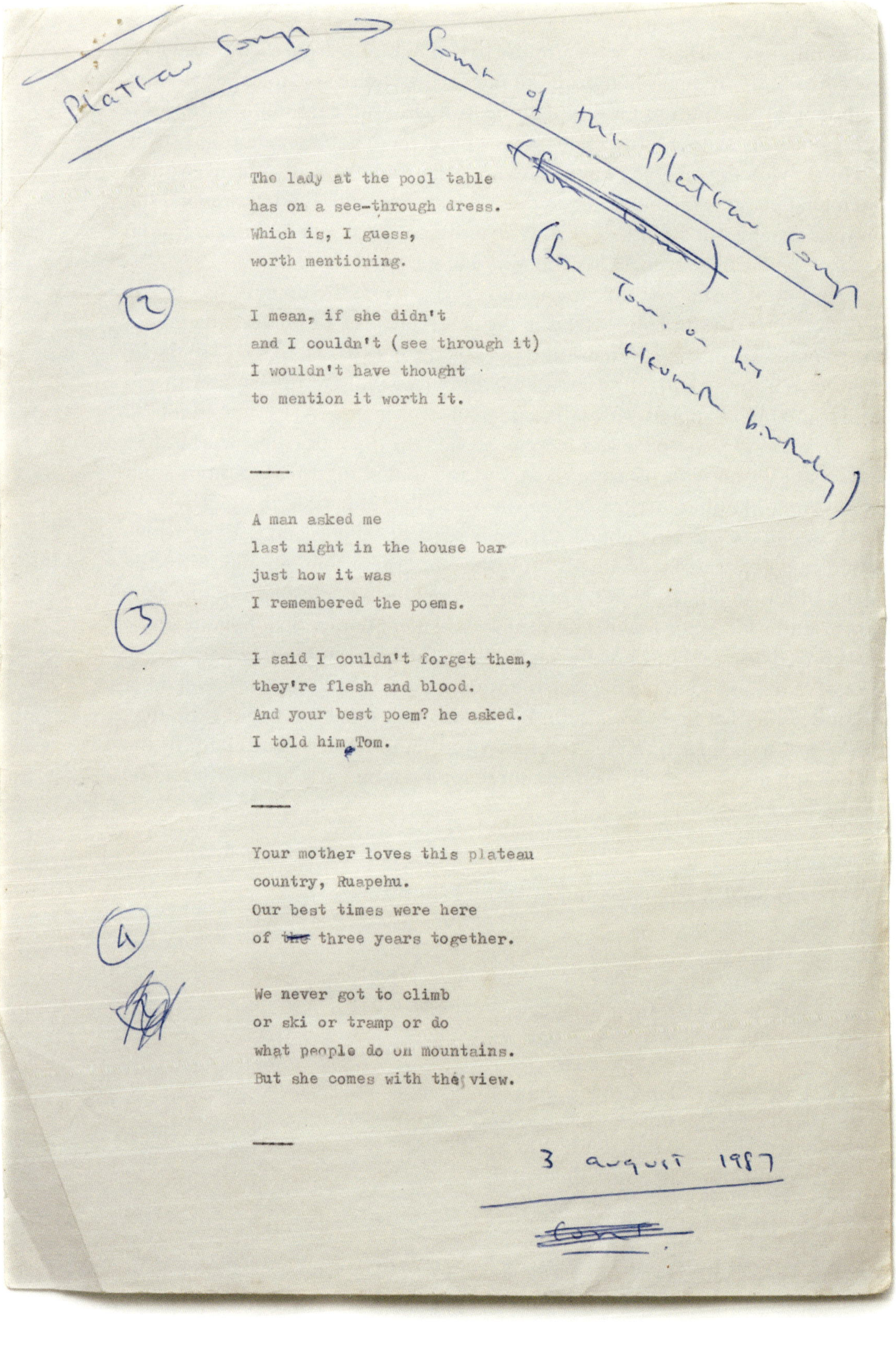

Plateau Songs → Some of the Plateau Songs

(for Tom, on his eleventh birthday)

The lady at the pool table
has on a see-through dress.
Which is, I guess,
worth mentioning.

(2)

I mean, if she didn't
and I couldn't (see through it)
I wouldn't have thought
to mention it worth it.

A man asked me
last night in the house bar
just how it was
I remembered the poems.

(3)

I said I couldn't forget them,
they're flesh and blood.
And your best poem? he asked.
I told him, Tom.

Your mother loves this plateau
country, Ruapehu.
Our best times were here
of ~~the~~ three years together.

(4)

We never got to climb
or ski or tramp or do
what people do on mountains.
But she comes with the view.

---

3 August 1987

A partial draft of 'Four Plateau Songs'

Four Plateau Songs
(for Tom, turning 11)

1
I climbed the mountain to learn
I had no need to be there,
took a room further down;
could not have gone further.

I spend the most, most days now
inside of a hotel room –
a distant dad, a dizzy man,
on the edge of a mountain.

2
The lady at the pool table
has on a see-through dress.
Which is, I guess,
worth mentioning.

I mean, if she didn't
and I couldn't (see through it)
I wouldn't have thought
to mention it worth it.

3
A man asked me
last night in the house bar
just how it was
I could remember poems.

I told him I could not forget them,
they're flesh and blood.
And your best poem? he asked.
I told him Tom.

4
Your mother loved this plateau
country, Ruapehu.
Our best times were here
of three years together.

We never got to climb
or ski or tramp or do
what people do on mountains.
But she comes with the view.

places

When I was quite young—I suppose about the age of twelve—I imagined what it would be like to be a poet full-time, to be living on your poems somehow. I had visions of living in the sort of places I ended up living in actually—quite vivid visions of that—and there were certain places I imagined I could live.

When I was fourteen, I actually got hold of the Waimea County Council in Nelson. By this time my relations in Nelson—farming people—had lost their ninety-nine-year lease on Rough Island on the Waimea Estuary, and I wanted to live over there or on Bird Island, which is just beyond. There were foundations for a house that had once been there, and I had a vision of fixing this place up, living there, writing my poems and acting as a caretaker. It didn't happen.

There was another time when I approached the then Takapuna Borough Council—now the North Shore City Council—about living in a gun emplacement on Back Beach past Castor Bay. It's on a reserve called John F. Kennedy Memorial Park and takes in that whole headland north of Castor Bay. This particular gun emplacement is still there—a big structure with great big wide open views. You could put windows in and it would be a brilliant place to live, looking straight out to Rangitoto. At full tide the fish used to come—you could see the snapper feeding off the reef just down below you. It was an incredible place and it could have worked, but again, I never got a reply from them.

Bottle Creek is on the Paremata Inlet in the Porirua Harbour. Porirua means two arms—one arm goes up to Porirua; the other arm goes up to Pauatahanui. That arm is sometimes referred to as the Pauatahanui Inlet, sometimes as the Paremata Inlet. Up there there was a bit of shoreline which was well away from the road because of the hills. It went between Shearers Point and the headland for perhaps a kilometre, and on that shoreline I found a place I wanted to rent. I was twenty-one. I had lived at Pukerua Bay then after that I'd gone back up north truck driving. In September of that year I'd come back down and stayed with Meg and Alistair, and while I was there I put the feelers out for a place. I liked

The boathouse at Mana, home from 1983 to 1996

the Paremata Inlet. One day Gregory Campbell—Alistair's son—and I had gone to get some fish and chips, and we went out to see if some friends of theirs—the Brockie family—were home, but they weren't. They lived in this little cottage which they rented from a man called Professor Monro, who lived up there on a big property. There were little cottages down the property, and I noticed an old one that seemed to be empty. Through Meg I met old Prof. and he said the place I'd seen was abandoned, so I said I'd be happy to live in it. So Prof. was my landlord—a great figure, bulls-eye glasses—an old retired professor of chemistry at Victoria University. They reckon when he retired they tested his laboratories for radioactivity and they all went off the screens.

Anyway, back to Bottle Creek. So I moved into this cottage. Prof. said, 'You can have it but I don't think I should charge you. It's too run down. Maybe if I put some work into it, then we can discuss it.' I said I'd be more comfortable if I gave him something. He said, 'We'll make it five shillings a week, okay?' Or was it half a crown a week—I have a feeling it was half a crown a week.

On the North Shore, a couple of my friends were—for want of another phrase—a sort of V8 crowd. I've often owned V8s myself—written a few poems about them—and there was an expression among the V8 boys that if you went to a good party, it would be 'good news from Battle Creek', or 'bad news from Battle Creek' if it wasn't. When I got down there, the place sort of demanded a name. I don't know how I started using it—I don't remember the moment I invented it—but I started referring to it as Bottle Creek. I bastardised it from Battle to Bottle.

As time went on, I'd be getting mail addressed to 'Sam Hunt, Bottle Creek, Paremata'. I was over at the Paremata Post Office—more often than not I'd row over in the dinghy and get the mail—and one of the women who worked there—she was a part-Samoan lady, Terri—said to me, 'I've been meaning to ask you, where does this Bottle Creek come from because we've been asked by the powers that be.' I said, 'Well, I'll tell you the story,' and she said, 'Any story will do.' I said, 'There was a battle here once and there used to be creek here, and someone put the two together and they started referring to it as Battle Creek. Over the years since then, with all the yachties, parties and things, the Battle's become Bottle, and that's the name I always heard when I moved here.' She said, 'That's good enough for me.' I actually found out that one of the first big challenges to government forces from Te Rangihaeata had been in the channel right in front of where I was living, so there had indeed been a battle. Anyway, I found out all about it, having made up the story to keep the authorities happy. I think there's a moral here and that is if you tell a lie long enough and convincingly enough, it will become the truth. And of course, now it's on the map.

Another reason I loved the word 'bottle' was a short story by Joseph Conrad called 'Youth', where the old sea captains sit around talking about ships that they've lost, and one great old captain tells a story about losing the first ship he ever had under his command, out in the Indian Ocean somewhere. He says, '… and I watched her go down like you see someone go that you know you'll never see again, pass the bottle.' I was so moved by that story—loved it so much—and I wrote a poem to Alistair Campbell which was called 'A Birthday Poem for Alistair'. I don't think it was ever published. One of the verses ends up 'it's been a battle, and no easy one, pass the bottle'—that's the line I always liked. I think I'm right in saying that Alistair's poem 'Drinking Horn'—which the Bottle Press published—came in response to the poem I'd sent him with that line. Every verse has 'pass the bottle' in it. So that ties the naming of the place with the printing thing.

If I'd never met Meg and Alistair, I suspect I would still have found Paremata—it was waiting for me. When you're young it seems such a long time but I was probably

Happy birthday, Sam.
As a notorious non-drinker
you might enjoy this poem.

Alistair

Drinking Horn

More urgently now
they come naked out of the wood -
the fugitive girls with platinum bodies
and vivid faces.
Their eyes are whiskey-coloured
and they have sex on the brain.
It is always the same . . .
Pass the bottle.

Because our heads have rolled
like bowler hats
under a spindly table
where a phone is ringing,
it would be easy to pretend
to the poor sex-mad girls
we are drunker than we think we are . . .
Pass the bottle.

Easy to pretend,
as we stare up at the miniskirts,
to a preference for maidenhair,
wet to the touch,
and water spilling over a lip
worn smooth as a girl's thigh . . .
I am dying of thirst.
Pass the bottle.

I believe we are going under
for the last time,
but I do not expect you to believe me,
and even if you did
it would not greatly matter -
the platinum girls
are well and truly rotten . . .
Pass the bottle.

Alistair Campbell

Bottle Creek / Paremata / Tuesday 14 August 1973

Dear Brian,

Midnight. Just arrived home from seeing you. And by Jesus it was good to see you, was it what! You know, sitting on the bridge there, smoking my first fag in fucking weeks, a closed-down tearooms one side of me, a dead rat in a trap the other side of me, the river clear and alive, the whole thing was so very good. Thanks, Brian, for a good couple of hours. Cheers.

Since then, I have driven across the Akatarawas, driving towards the west; toward the evening; towards the light. That little beachbuggy, you know, she climbed and climbed and loved it! yes, and so did I. I couldn't help stopping all the way up (sd. bishop to actress).

Once on the sunset slopes, I turned the engine off and coasted, quite literally, westward and sunward to the coast.

I had dinner with friends tonight, Prue and Jerry Ursell. Good people, very good too to see them after a long time. Jerry advised me against the Hill Road tonight, saying What if I broke down? Anyway, despite Jerry and all that, I took the Hill Road, across from Paekakariki to Pauatahanui, the moon full and wild. It's one life Brian, and a fucking beauty.

Bottle Creek now as I write, sea slapping away there under my house. All is so insubstantial, floorboards rotting - but, as you said (and so rivght) - we're camping here. I love this little place though, I do. All that I've done today has been so good. To write my PARIHAKA poem for you, drive across Moonshine, later the Akatarawas, south; then back from the west coast to Pauatahanui; up the inlet, Bottle Creek that I named myself. And that is good. Good, to end up at home, here, Bottle Creek, that had no name until I came to live here. Others live here now. They call it "Bottle Creek". It is a name for them.

For me it is a reality. I love it as such. Waves banging the bows. Bottle Creek sends its love. And so do I.

only there eight years, from September '67 until after I'd come back from that mini Burns Fellowship in Dunedin, about May 1976. After the cottage I rented a boatshed, also at Bottle Creek, but we needed something bigger because Kristin, my girlfriend, was about to have a baby. We found a new place—it was named before we got there—Battle Hill, so Bottle to Battle already. It was named Battle Hill in 1846, nothing to do with me. Then we lived at Death's Corner, which was also named well before I got there, so Bottle to Battle to Death. Death's Corner was a big old rambling homestead, the old Death homestead. Darky Death was the ghost who used to inhabit that place. I wrote a poem called 'Drunkard's Garden' in tribute to him. They were the three places where Kristin and I lived while we were together, and I wrote a poem about them: 'From Bottle to Battle to Death'. They were all great places and we had some great times there, maybe some harrowing times too.

Bottle to Battle to Death

From Bottle to Battle to Death,
places where we lived from
meeting up one crazy night to
splitting up – a child in tow –
one nightmare of an afternoon.

Bottle Creek was our first home,
a boathouse perched on stilts.
The heron thought us one of them.
We paced the mudflats; full tide, swam:
no place (they said) to bring a baby up in.

To Battle Hill where once, one
hundred years before you or I were born,
a poet of a chief held back the Poms.
He let the land fight for him.
Our child was born here, Tom.

Those days, some days, were good,
the nappies flapping at the clouds,
the clouds crash-landing on the hills.
And white as mushrooms on the slopes,
the sheep; at lambing-time, the hawk.

We gave our child Kahu for
a second name, in honour of that hawk.

Our silences invaded us –
the dark hills, sky, the hovering.
It was, for us, an end of talk.

The move then down the valley,
back beside the estuary, the ancient
homestead, Death (and not D' Ath).
We didn't stand a chance.
We stalked each other, minute by minute.

I would watch the shy pukeko. They
would run out on the road, crazy as
the clouds that charged the hills.
The cars would always win the game.
Pukeko dead, a dull blue flame.

And then, of course, there was you.
And to say I loved you was true.
And that I hated you was true.
I thought though, if we lie down,
lie down low, we may come through.

Instead, minute by minute, we stalked
each other out. Sometimes we walked
the hills together, Tom in the back-pack,
the dog forever chasing sticks.
And then an afternoon, quite casually, I talked

of 'going our own ways'. I can't
remember now what brought me to it.
Maybe you said, we can't go on this way.
Or, maybe best we call it all a day.
I don't know now. But you went away.

Then Kristin and I separated and I lived all over the place but for a period in Wellington city. After that I moved back out to the inlet and that's when I bought the boathouse in Mana. When Tom was starting to get a little bit older he could travel on the train on his own—the unit as they call it in Wellington—and I'd meet him either at Paremata or Mana. The nice thing about Paremata Station was that I could go over in the dinghy, pull up underneath the railway bridge at Paremata and wander along to the station to meet him. Then we'd wander back to the dinghy and off to the boathouse—it was great.

At Battle Hill, 1976

On the Mana boathouse jetty—low tide

Choosing the place to live is part of the process of finding the silence. Also, I've got to admit that I was drawn by the romantic notion of living in a boatshed. I've always loved the sea, and it struck me as a pretty good place for a poet to live. You know those lovely lines of Alistair Campbell's 'Wild Honey':

> Meg's loveliness ... In that absurd boatshed
> how it glowed, while the tide chuckled and slapped
> below us – God, how she glowed! ... Wild honey.

Boatsheds are good places.

I never had any inclination whatever—when I was a young man in my twenties—to join a lot of my contemporaries and get married and move to a house on the hill. I didn't get married and I remain not married—I don't believe in marriage—it's not one of the sacraments I hold dear—but I appreciate it for other people. I live with my son Alf and that I love—I love it intensely—but I find it very difficult to live full-time with a woman. That's no reflection on the woman involved—it just doesn't suit me. If there's a woman I'm close to, I look forward greatly to seeing her and I hope she looks forward to seeing me, but to have that person there all the time, and all the small bits of their life too—I find it very distracting.

None of these moves were made with this deliberate thing in the forefront of my mind, 'I must have a place which is good for composing poems'—I'm not quite as precious as that. But the process is all part of it—and I'm very aware of it—and I would be very unhappy to be going into a situation which is alien to that. People have said, 'How do you find these places right by the water where there's no one around?' I suppose you learn how to look, always have your eye out.

Travelling around New Zealand has pretty much always been a pleasure for me. I'm not really interested in travelling to a whole lot of other places. I like peanut butter thick on my toast, don't like it spread too thin. One of the things I became aware of from a very early age of travelling—I hit the road when I was twelve, hitch-hiking up to see my grandfather in the North—it was different world then, a twelve year old could go hitch-hiking—was that New Zealand is basically a bigger version of all those small towns. It's that old adage of finding the universe in a grain of sand—if you can understand what's going on in this town, you can probably understand a lot more than just that.

That feeling-of-being-in-the-country

When you stop at some small country town
and some local –
after you've complimented them on their town –
says We like it it's a good community

you think of that group of people
for whom this place is town,
Reporoa, say,

everyone creating their own sort of light
throwing it out their kind of way
and you think of that community
and the communion of saints.

I never felt less
like wearing dark glasses
than in Reporoa this morning.

I've always felt very happy in small towns—they've played an important part in my life. I'm lucky that I can go to those small places and generally get as good a sized audience as I would in a city because people know what's going on. Publicity's easier too—there's one publication, one radio station maybe. The good thing for me is that there are a hell of a lot more smaller towns than big towns in New Zealand. I could never claim to have done a show in every town in New Zealand but I've been to most of them.

An important part of my touring has been the high schools. That's had a lot to do with my love for those small towns. I've had some wonderful experiences that have been sometimes sad. I remember one small town where I was doing a show at the high school during the day and the pub at night—well that school had just had three teenage suicides within the last month. The town was reeling, understandably—they'd lost three of their brightest, loveliest kids who had just hit the wall. That whole feeling of grief and being stunned was still palpable that night at the pub. It was a full house—the parents of at least one of the young people who'd killed themselves were there—and I felt deeply moved by it. It wasn't just a matter of passing through—sometimes people get the image of the itinerant performer not really touching lives or being touched by lives.

That poem of mine 'Old Flames' was a result of that visit. When I left the town the following day, I stopped at Tarras and had a lovely conversation with the woman who ran the Four Square. We got talking about what had been happening down the road at this high school and she said to me, 'Well Sam, I'll tell you one thing, some fires you can't put out.' I didn't say thank you for the line but the next day I wrote 'Old Flames'.

Old Flames

The cabbage tree was, they said,
dead. There was nothing they
or anyone could do
now or any day –
how sorry they
were, and sad.

But the cabbage tree heard them –
they never noticed
it shaking its head:
it shook it so hard
stars were said to have spread
from where the cabbage tree stood:

a blossoming, new constellation
across that night sky south.
Someone said just
yesterday,
some fires
you can't put out.

So she gave me the poem. A lot of the poems that I have made up have been given to me by the small towns, the small communities. I would so far rather be driving into a small town than into a big city that just goes suburb after suburb after suburb, which I find very depressing. If small towns are one of my great loves, then suburbia is one of my great hates. The great Baxter poem 'The Ballad of Calvary Street' says 'Why hammer nails? Why give no change?'

It's not that I've ever deliberately chosen to write poems with small-town settings, but the fact is that a lot of the poems have come from there and my sort of poems generally reflect where I am, in both physical and other senses. One of the most productive times and places for writing poems is a small-town motel the next day after you've done your thing. The next morning you can take your time drinking cups of coffee and working on a poem—it's a good time. You can find all the different sorts of people in a small town and it's easy—it's not like going to some big suburb, an affluent suburb, where you're not going to meet many people who are on the dole or are labourers. In a small town, especially doing a show there, you get that complete cross-section of humanity, which is what it's all about. In terms of doing a show, the sort of response you get is that much more real because it's not just from a whole lot of people who are roughly equal in standing or status or education or background—you've got the whole range. People deal on a human level basically, and you're not just another face in the crowd. Nor is anyone else. You know who people are, and there's a greater sense of dignity, I think, in a small town.

I don't live in a town, but the town that I'm closest to in an emotional sense rather than a physical sense is Paparoa, which is where I collect my mail and do my shopping. It's a good town, and there are all sorts of people—there are Brethrens, dope dealers, one of the Mr Asia gang was discovered still living here, and there's everyone else. I don't just mean the darker side—it's a good community. You do develop some very important bonds—friendships. I like it, I know people's names. It sounds corny to say it but it's true, they look after you. They know Alf's learning the guitar: 'How's it going? Are you putting in your practice? You're not playing too loud for your old dad?' You walk down the street and it has everything you need—there's a pub and a store, a café. It's a beautiful town in a little valley with the Paparoa River running through it.

I would say that the people and the places have been a source of inspiration. I know I talk about poems coming from the silence, but the actual subject matter or the setting of the poem would often be in such a place, even if it's just in my mind. I love that line of Ezra Pound's at the end of one of his cantos:

> ... o world my poems were written for five people o world I pity you,
> you do not know these five people

If I'd been going from city to city like an international act—going to the big arenas every night—I wouldn't still be performing because I would've been bored shitless. I'm not anti-city—I love a good city. I love New York. I love Melbourne. I love Wellington and Dunedin. The grey area where I have my problems is the suburbs. I'm claustrophobic, and my biggest attacks can come on me when I'm lost in some suburb somewhere. And if I have claustrophobic dreams, it's not about being locked in a tunnel—it's being lost in the suburbs.

Jimmy Vernon's house, Hunterville

Jimmy Vernon

Remember Jimmy Vernon,
what came of him?
Thought then of all
the boys from Hunterville,
Jimmy, Untamed Freddy and the Boys,
Heaven bent and mad as Hell.

They shacked up just out of town
in what was a farmhouse once.
When we met up in '71,
Jimmy, Untamed Freddy and the Boys,
girlfriends and kids,
were shacking in the kitchen:

a cold winter, '71, the house
good firewood! and the landlord
never had a house to call a house
to throw them out of anyway.
There was nothing to be done –
that kitchen was home.

Remember Jimmy Vernon then,
what came of him?
The barman, polishing a glass,
told me the rest:
killed on the level-crossing,
July or August last.

He nodded out the window
to the line that cuts the town in two –
the line Jimmy Vernon
crossed
but never saw the signals flash.
A cold winter, Jimmy, a good bash.

Robin White, Sam Hunt at the Portobello Pub, *1978*

PULL

company in the dark nights

I feel blessed to take on the task of keeping other poets' poems alive, particularly other New Zealand poets. If I'm doing a show and suddenly start thinking about something like 'The Magpies', I can just go into it. People, like Glover, who write poems, they're touching something which is beyond ordinary touch—it's something very special. And they don't always—when it's happening around them—realise it. It's only posterity that will confirm it for them. It's humbling I reckon.

When James K. Baxter wrote, in October 1965 in New Zealand, 'The Gunner's Lament', in the same month—the same week as far as I can work out, maybe even the same day—a young Bob Dylan was writing a poem called 'John Brown', which is on the same subject and with the same verse structure, in New York. It's all to do with the same war and looking in the face of the enemy and realising you're the same person. That's sort of tangible proof of the magic of poems.

It makes complete sense to me if I'm doing a show to do cover versions, if you like, of my greats. I love the fact that there are so many songs and poems out there and I notice with interest that the poets whose work I know enough to be able to say this about feel the same. For example Bob Dylan's knowledge of the American songbook and of American poetry is apparently encyclopaedic—it becomes very clear. It's lovely that, and I think to have that knowledge and awareness of what the people who have gone before us have said is all part of the person standing on stage delivering. There's no such thing as a new act—if it's any good it's more than just new, it's also ancient. I would not want to go out on stage for the two halves and just do all my own stuff—I could—but that's not what it is about. It's about what I hope is a more interesting picture than that. And week by week new poems come along. A younger poet has just sent me a bunch of poems, and I did one of his poems on a radio broadcast this morning, about his kids—a great poem, which enters the canon, if you like.

I'm aware of the tradition. When I was younger I probably would have said to let that look after itself, and I would still say much that same. The only thing as I've got older is that I am more aware of company in the dark nights, I can hear the rattling of bones. Late last night I was reading a wonderful poem of Yeats's called 'Hound Voice'. It's a voice that has always been there—when that poem was a brand new poem and Yeats had just finished it and wrote out the final copy, I can tell you that poem would have been a new poem, but also as old as time, as old as time. You are part of a big sea wind that blows in and that has been blowing for a long time and when you smell the salt and you notice the sea wind and start hearing the poems.

JAMES K. BAXTER

I first met Jim Baxter when I was 19 years old. I was staying with Meg and Alistair Campbell, and Alistair on numerous occasions said, 'We must get Jim around, I would love you to meet him.' I didn't want to be a groupie, but anyway it was decided that there was going to be a party. I was arranging to rent a cottage in Pukerua Bay and I had to go out to Ngaio to see the people who owned it—in the same suburb in which Jim and Jacquie Baxter lived. I got onto the train in Wellington to go out on the Johnsonville line and a postman got on. He was reading *Time* magazine. It was pre the long hair so he had short back and sides, and I was sitting there and he looked across to me and said. 'Gidday!' I was just going to say, 'You're Jim Baxter, aren't you,' and a woman who had witnessed this said, 'Oh yes, that is Louis Johnson.' Jim never forgot that. Lou was quite well known in Wellington then—he used to write in the evening paper and he was on television quite a bit so he was quite a well-known figure, as was Jim, I suppose. So it was a great crack-up as they were old friends and because both were very generous men.

About two days later a party happened where we met again and had an interesting time. He was in Ngaio—he had come back from being down in Otago with the Burns Fellowship—and we arranged to meet up. We had a good afternoon and he said to me, 'I've been having these dreams.' He had a vision and he told me that he had to go to Jerusalem. I was one among many people that he would have told that at the time, and he wrote about it too. He said, 'Would you like to come with me to Jerusalem, up the Wanganui River, set up some sort of place to live and make it possible for others?' He told me what he had in mind. I said, 'I'll come up and see you,' which I actually never did, though I did after he had died. I also said, 'I need to find my own Jerusalem, Jim.'

I didn't have a telephone at Bottle Creek, but my neighbour and friend along the shoreline, Jill Tenant, did and she was a contact number for me. The next day Jill came along the beach quite excited and said, 'Jim Baxter's on the phone for you.' I just couldn't get my head around the thought of Jim being on a phone—the two just didn't go together. So I went along and he said, 'Hello Sam, how's the

James K. Baxter at a poetry reading with Sam Hunt, Massey University, 1971

old cabbage tree today?' I answered, 'Good. I've been thinking that was a good session yesterday.' He answered, 'You are right. I'm ringing to say how right you are, we've all got to find our own Jerusalem, but you always know where I am.' That was lovely, and that was the nature of Jim Baxter.

In 1966 Baxter published *Pig Island Letters*, which contained some of the great, great poems—as all his books do—and one of the lesser individual poems was part of the sequence 'Pig Island Letters'. In that particular poem he's got the line 'Love is not valued much in Pig Island.' As a young man in my early twenties, I didn't really agree with that. I suppose I was in love with the notion of romantic love—still am. So I wrote a poem in reply, which I posted off to Jim—this must have been after his second year of the Burns Fellowship in Dunedin. It was called 'Reply to a Pig Island Letter', and that was where the correspondence sort of kicked off. It's not a very good poem, but I was saying that love is valued—is thriving, in fact—in Pig Island. It's never been in a book of poems of mine, but Jim liked it—maybe he was just being kind. In response to that poem came 'Letter to Sam Hunt'.

OPPOSITE *The original of James K. Baxter's 'Letter to Sam Hunt'*

LETTER TO SAM HUNT

Dear Sam, I thank you for your letter
And for the poem too, much better
To look at than the dreary words
I day by day excrete like turds
To help the Catholic bourgeoisie
To bear their own insanity;
And if in Paremata you
Should find a weta in your shoe,
Ugly, hard-shelled, with snapping jaws,
A Hitler who has lost his cause,
Don't hit it with a shovel - No,
Christen it JIM and let it go.

Though it may serve no good, in rhyme,
To look back on the fucking-time,
I do recall one evening, drunk
In Devonport on Dally plonk,
Endangering my balls and marriage
With someone's darling in a garage,
Upright and groaning, breaking eggs
Until the yolk ran down her legs, -
One of the best of Venus' nuns,
A girl with tits like ack-ack guns
Who sighed and screwed and screwed and sighed
While her grim husband sat inside
The house and meditated death
For her and me with every breath,
Journalist, tombstone-maker, or
Some other kind of social whore.
Last year we met again and she
Not screwing sighed and looked at me,
A swaddled deathshead old and dry,
But there was life in that blue eye.

'Honey,' I said, 'you're thinking of
Another time when love was love.'

'You've struck it, brother,' she replied,
'But now I find the gap inside
Is cold and dark and hard to carry
And Buddha is the man I marry;
He teaches me that love is love
Only when it's past thinking of.'

Dear Sam, if you are twenty-two,
Why should I foist my gall on you?
The answer is that poets live
By a refusal to forgive
The mighty Bog of social shit
That has no use for sex or wit
Or art or hope, but simply is
Internally its own Abyss;
At twenty-two or forty-one
You need your gumboots and a gun.

Sam Hunt, Sam Hunt, Sam Hunt, Sam Hunt,
The housewife with her oyster cunt
Has pissed upon what might have been
Lively, original and green,
The old pohutukawa Tree
With hairy ballocks on its knee.
The Pill, the Rags, the Summer Sale,
Put Venus and her tribe in jail
Till every fuck's a coffin-nail;
Her husband, that sad pudding-head,
Will pull himself each night in bed
Softly, for fear he'll wake the Dead,
And teach his children how to lick
The Boss's arse and not be sick, -
Not that I blame the poor blind bitch
Who hoped that she would strike it rich
But saw her pretty flowers wilt,
Her cunt turn into a patchwork quilt,
Her handsome Prince become a Frog,
And drowned herself in the Social Bog.

But I must go my own way still
Across Death Brig and up Skull Hill
To learn the science of our grief
Conversing with the Impenitent Thief,
The one unique left-handed saint
Who knows why we must write and paint.
He teaches me that Sophocles
Heard in the thunder of Greek seas
On beaches grey with ambergris,
In the recoiling serpent hiss
A voice proclaiming to the land
That men are banks of broken sand,
And various other things that I
May put in plays before I die.

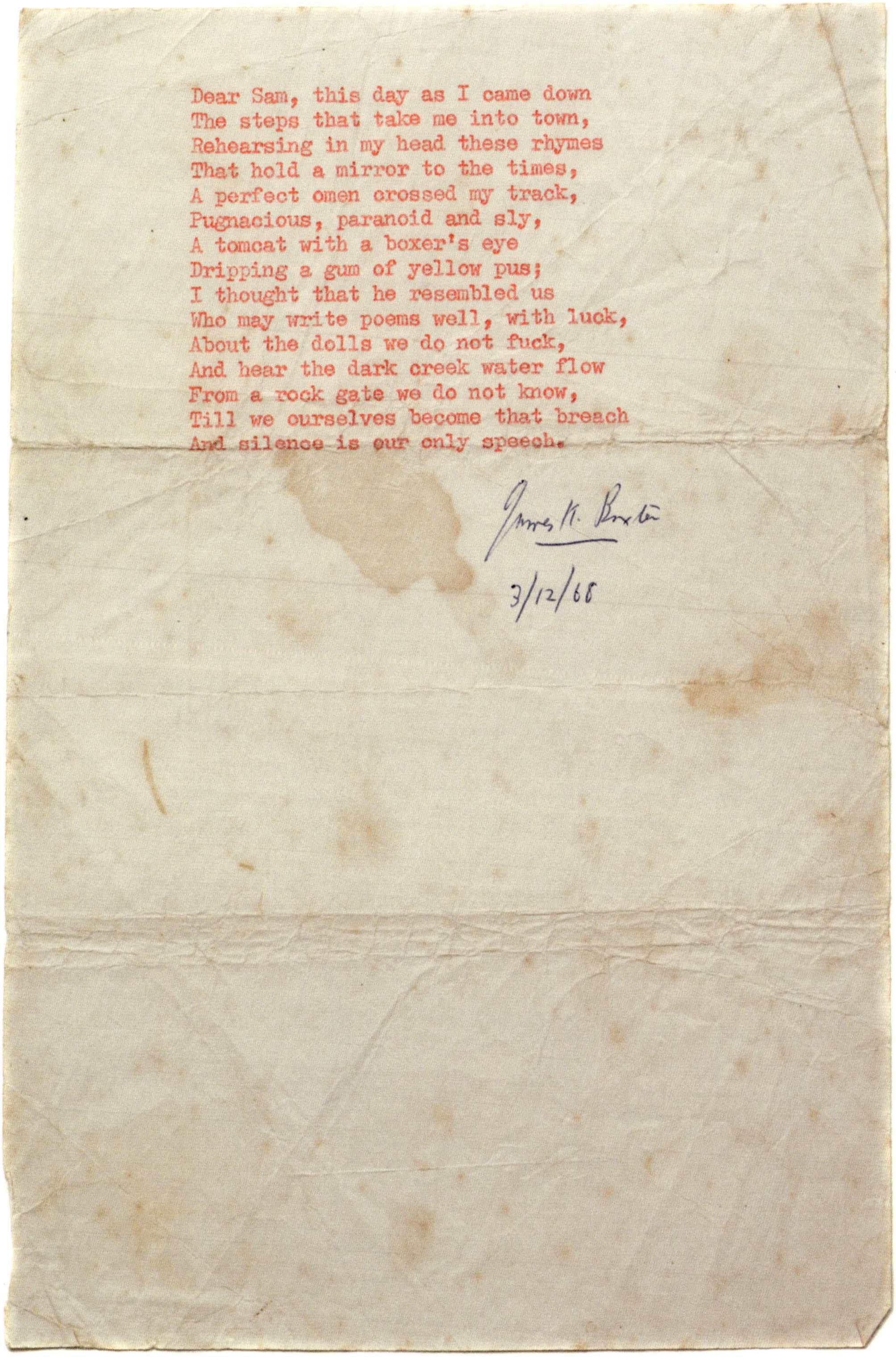

Dear Sam, this day as I came down
The steps that take me into town,
Rehearsing in my head these rhymes
That hold a mirror to the times,
A perfect omen crossed my track,
Pugnacious, paranoid and sly,
A tomcat with a boxer's eye
Dripping a gum of yellow pus;
I thought that he resembled us
Who may write poems well, with luck,
About the dolls we do not fuck,
And hear the dark creek water flow
From a rock gate we do not know,
Till we ourselves become that breach
And silence is our only speech.

James K. Baxter

3/12/68

Then I responded with 'Letter to Jerusalem 1', which has been published in my Collected Poems. As I recall, 'Kumara Poem' came back after that one.

Letter to Jerusalem 1

1
Over the years I've pinned
faith on many women,
given them all I owned
to be their kind of man

and now do little more
than please their each sweet whim:
I'm pushing twenty-four
in need of guidance, Jim:

because all I know —
all cuff and rotten breath
black-eyed and bloodshot now —
is that I need a bath

in an Akitio spring,
clamber wet the autumn
riverbanks, a pilgrim
towards Jerusalem.

2.
Impossible in talk
or verses to resolve
these riddles that will take
me to the grave to solve.

I've asked your contemporaries
the answers and the facts
but find their hang-up is
the over-forty fuck.

Odd enough, I found more out
in a Sunday newspaper
double-page splurge about
a man who found a pauper

propped inside himself, a stubble-
faced and faceless man;
how in his steps he stumbled
towards Jerusalem.

3
But you see I'm far
from any answers yet.
But that's what I'm after
with the toe-jam and sweat.

With these wiped away
it's all too easy
to think that all's OK:
a game of Happy Family,

a plate-glass harbour view,
regular teaching job
and regular screw,
the occasional jab;

holidays hire a jet-boat
return to Oblivion. . . .
I think the wiser bet
is one-way to Jerusalem.

Kumara Poem
(for Sam Hunt)

Too many and too much,
the people and the happenings
left standing like dry bramble
when the fire eats inside it;
if there is a testament
it will never now be written
by this gun-shy ex-poet,

nevertheless, Fog-Arse,
I love you, man. The nun's cows
flap their slack udders out
there in the wet grass; Zema
with her shirt outside her jeans
is cooking rolled oats in a little
pot, and humming her own tune;

and this is Hiruharama …
To be a bad Dad, Sam,
with a house of wild friends,
so gentle the day, so quiet
the rain beginning to fall
and the smoke beginning to rise
from the cigarettes in the rooms,

that the slipped disc in my spine
hardly ticks; and I forget
the song of Heremaia
raving among the mildewed
smashed houses where the kehua
stands at noon – 'Aue, aue
kua mate Te Atua!' –

All of the students who get here
in family Jaguars or
with swollen feet, say – 'Man,
it's bad! I've blown my mind;
I need …' They don't know what,
and I don't either; except maybe
the same notes in a different tune;

but up at the old house
nobody is slamming cards
on the table at 4 a.m.
and shouting – 'Holy fuck!' –
there I can be poor at last
and even sleep for two hours
in a Maori cloud. You know, Sam,

my feet are nailed here to the ground,
the house of words has fallen down,
and this old kumara will rot
while the young red ones grow slowly
out of his gut … What is it
to lose the I, the instrument
we made our own sod hutch with?

'Kua mate Te Atua' –
the great ghost has gone
with his brandy and canticles;
down here, down low, it is to
eat the bread a girl
baked for herself and us
with sixty scars on her arms.

[James K. Baxter]

I'm not sure of the sequence here but I think I then wrote 'Letter to Jerusalem 2', in which I adopted the heroic couplets that Baxter had used in 'Letter to Sam Hunt'. It wasn't bang, bang, bang—there were sometimes months in between. But usually when I bounced one down the table at him, there would be a reply pretty quickly. It was a good rally.

Letter to Jerusalem 2

On the skyline of the Kaiwhara hills,
Gill, a mother to the kids on pills
Keeps open house, sends you her love.
Johnny too, who may forget to leave
For work some mornings in the woolstore
Sits drinking in the sun outside the door:
Tall buildings no bigger than blocks on the floor,
Wellington afloat on the harbour haze … .
You think of how most men spend their days
In offices as cramped as elevators —
Their wish, to be heading Heavenwards,
'Up in the world' to use their words!
The law they all ignore, of gravity,
My friends at Kaiwhara and I
Observe in this old house against the sky …
The Fall. Whatever. The sun on the sea.
Too much of this good life, I'll go dry!

Summer coming, Sylvia and I will sleep
Together often in the sun—and slip
A long way off, a long way from the beat
And hurt of words. And wake, carnal with heat.

I got round to thinking I'd better reply,
I owe you a letter, Old Father Sky,
Tell you what I'm up to. I hitch-hiked out
This afternoon to Bottle Creek,
Could easily have made it with the chick
Who picked me up: I've little doubt
She'd very much fancy a denim lout —
A little rougher than her easy-action
Husband who fails to bring her on.
She went out of her way, drove me right home.
I didn't try. Instead, told her this poem
I'm now writing down.

Did I want to travel?
She asked, and nearly slid on the gravel
When I told her my only ambition
Was to make a perfect act of contrition,
And when I grew up, to be a moonshiner
Whisky-mad and bare-back on the hills,
And to fart as loud as an ocean-liner.

But the world, old cock, is hard on my heels.
The truth is, Jim, the Education Board
Is gunning me down with a 3-year bond
To teach young kids a cursive script
Tidy as a row of angels' holes,
To teach the kids that if they have to shit
To clean up afterwards and keep clean souls.

It's hard, but there we are! I think by now
You'll have the message strong. I don't know how,
But very soon I'm off outside to join
Johnny for a beer … and toss a coin
Late on some summer afternoon.
Whichever way it falls, I'll see you soon.

When the news of Baxter's death came, I was on the Kaipara Harbour—funnily enough, near where I live today. I was with my mother this particular day, Labour Day 1972, and we'd decided to go for a drive up there from Auckland. We walked into the pub at Kaukapakapa wanting to buy some beer to take away, and the eleven o'clock news came on, on the La Gloria radio above the bar. The news came that the poet James K. Baxter was dead, and of course I was stunned as was everyone else. I remember *The Dominion* newspaper had a billboard: *James K. Baxter 1926–1972, friend.* He was a great friend to me, a very dear friend and a man whose company I loved. I remember, hearing the news of his death, the barman saying, 'What was it you wanted, mate?'—I was thinking, 'A poem, he still owes me one, one last bit of correspondence.'

A week or two later, when I got back to where I lived at Bottle Creek, I rowed across in the dinghy to the then Paremata Post Office to collect the mail which had accumulated during the time I'd been away. I was expecting a bit of mail, the odd bill. The old inevitable handwriting was there, addressed to 'Sam Hunt, Bottle Creek, Paremata'. He got the last poem in—a beautiful poem called 'Jerusalem Blues 2'.

He got me—the old bastard got me, and so that was the end of—well I won't say the end of a friendship because the poems go on and go on forever. He was an extraordinary poet. I look at photographs and realise how young he was. I'm sixty-two now. Jim was only forty-six—you're hardly out of school by forty-six.

Jerusalem Blues 2

An old man with a smoke,
I sit in the transport shelter
where the flies buzz in and out,
watching the crates and mailbags;
it's cool in here, Sam,
the bracken shoots curl up
and my head is full of holes
like the leather cuffs on my coat,

and if my feet are bare
and the hair hangs down my back –
well, is it so wild an omen
for the surburban men
and their wives who swallow pills
and their daughters who smoke pot?
All that my nerves can tell me
is that the sun is hot.

And over in the cottage
Karl has made some coffee;
soon I'll take out my beads,
sweat-stained and dark with use
from rubbing through my fingers
like poems or self-abuse,
and ramble through the Mysteries
old as the griefs of the Jews,

and I'll confess that surely
the over-forty fuck
touches my mind when Nikki
goes down to have a wash
in the arms of the taniwha
with her little bulging puku
and her hair like a midnight cloud,
but the sandflies nip my ankle

and it's enough for this
dead man to rest his head

for a minute on her tits
and tell her she looks fabulous –
'He tino pai te kai,
he tino pai te ra,
he tino pai te mate' –
no, it is not a trip,

you can hear the children yelling
on the dirt road of the pa –
fair enough – now Peter,
not long out of the bin,
an eagle who stares at the sun,
has come to sit beside me –
'You're writing a poem, Hemi?
Well, it's about time' –

I leave him to talk to the drive
and head back for a shit –
no angel with a scroll,
no news from thunder mountain,
no journey at all to make,
just a knife to cut open
the loaf of Maori bread
that goes to feed my gut.

[James K. Baxter]

There is a very revealing story about Baxter, quite a revealing story I always thought. This was in 1971, about a year before he died, and there was the New Zealand University Students Association Arts Festival at Massey in Palmerston North. Baxter and I were on the bill together for a big afternoon performance, which was a marathon. Anyway, I got off to Palmerston North the night before the gig, got on the piss that night, and lost any poems and notes that I had. I'd been on the road a bit but this was still quite early days for me, so I still used my notes and bits of poems. I lost the whole bloody lot and never saw them again. Anyway, I arrived at the venue still quite confident that I would manage, that I had enough in my memory banks that hadn't been destroyed by alcohol the night before. Jim arrived with his acolytes—a couple of Catholic priests—Jim Kebble and some other fellow, with Jim Kebble carrying quite a few of Jim's books for the reading. We were getting ready to go on stage and Jim Baxter said to me, 'Where're your poems?' I said, 'They're all up here, Jim.' Do you know what he did? He got Kebble to take his books back to the car. It can't be completely true as there's a photograph of us both on that occasion with Jim up reading (see page 84), and I'm in the background. From my memory, though, he did most of that without notes.

The Massey show was the only time we ever went on stage together. He really enjoyed it and he was really enthusiastic about it, and there was talk about doing some other things. I didn't realise it at the time but there was an element of trailblazing in what I was doing—the kind of performing I was doing hadn't been done in New Zealand or anywhere else for that matter, as far as I can work out.

I remember writing a poem after he died called 'Notes from a Journey', which was addressed to Hone Tuwhare.

Notes from a Journey
(for Hone)

When I left Wanganui
(you and Eve asleep still
low under canvas) my pilgrimage
was northward up
the river of the three taniwha

The sun shone; every little
township had its one-way bridge.
By midday, man, it seemed
a month instead of
half a day since leaving

Three o'clock that afternoon
I picked up three local boys,
Tawe, Gabriel, Andrew;
drove them through
Pipiriki out to Raetihi

They told me of Hemi, how
a month ago he walked
the whole way out on foot
'27 bloody miles of it!'
He died soon after that

'What if we meet old Hemi
around the next bend?' I asked.
'Let the bugger walk it'
one boy laughed. I turned
laughing with him

His face was dust and tears.
I passed him the bottle,
double declutching,
chopping down the gears.
It was a steep, slow climb.

Often I almost expected to come around a corner and see him padding along. He used to walk amazing distances. I think one time he walked out to Paremata when I was in Bottle Creek. I know he definitely walked from Porirua, because he called in to see one of his old friends on the way at the old Nolan Homestead, old Des Nolan, a Union man. He would walk between towns.

ALISTAIR AND MEG CAMPBELL

I had an introduction to Alistair by my schoolteacher Ken Arvidson, who knew my love for Alistair's work. Ken said to me one holidays (I was going down to the South Island), 'If you're in Wellington, you should look up Alistair Campbell. I'll drop him a line.' I hitch-hiked down—I remember I was 15, it was the August holidays and I was meant to be studying for exams, but I was studying by going to check the master out. I got a very wet, wild day in Cook Strait. Coming out to the coast on Highway 1, the sea was just crashing in. When I got put off at Pukerua Bay, I went and sheltered at the store and I said to the woman, who years later became a good friend, 'Does Alistair Campbell live around here?' She pointed up to a headland which was jutting out into the storm. You couldn't see Kapiti Island, there was rain and wind coming in, but you could just see a house. 'That's their place.' It was almost like a lighthouse at the end of a headland—not tall like a lighthouse but the same position. In fact, that site was used way before they ever built there by whalers as a whale-sighting spot. It was a long walk up there and I knocked on the door and met Meg and Alistair. They became my southern family and at different times I stayed with them and they stayed with us up in Auckland. We just got on so well. I never felt I was a literary person but I loved poems, and what I loved about Meg and Alistair is that, between them, they had such a vast reading. Alistair introduced me to a lot of the poets whose work he admired, people like George Mackay Brown. And Theodore Roethke, James Wright. Mum hadn't found those American poets, so now I could introduce her to them. Alistair had a very keen ear, and a very keen eye too—his day job at that time was as an editor of school publications. We had a lot of good times—a lot of laughter, as Meg says in her poem 'Meeting Sam Hunt'—the line about laughing until our eyes fell out.

Alistair was born, if I've got it right, in 1925, so he was twenty-one years older than me. When I lived in the last house in south Pukerua Bay in 1966, when I was

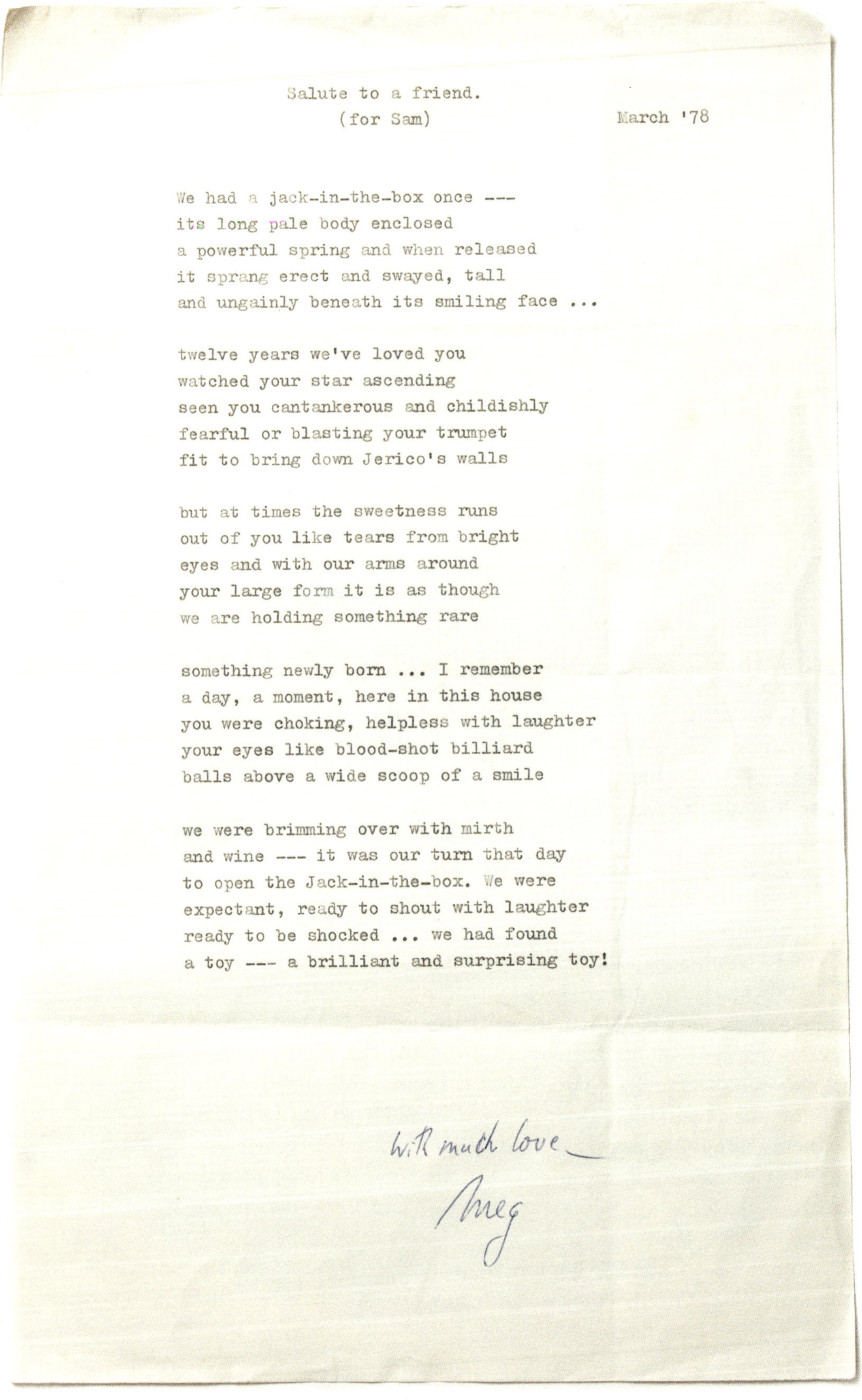

Salute to a friend.
(for Sam) March '78

We had a jack-in-the-box once ---
its long pale body enclosed
a powerful spring and when released
it sprang erect and swayed, tall
and ungainly beneath its smiling face ...

twelve years we've loved you
watched your star ascending
seen you cantankerous and childishly
fearful or blasting your trumpet
fit to bring down Jerico's walls

but at times the sweetness runs
out of you like tears from bright
eyes and with our arms around
your large form it is as though
we are holding something rare

something newly born ... I remember
a day, a moment, here in this house
you were choking, helpless with laughter
your eyes like blood-shot billiard
balls above a wide scoop of a smile

we were brimming over with mirth
and wine --- it was our turn that day
to open the Jack-in-the-box. We were
expectant, ready to shout with laughter
ready to be shocked ... we had found
a toy --- a brilliant and surprising toy!

With much love —
Meg

Poem by Meg Campbell

turning twenty, Alistair had a year for great poems, like 'Why Don't You Talk To Me?' and 'Mermaid For Sam Hunt'—'A mermaid is my gift to you dear friend...' He was having a prolific time. I remember one time when he came down to see me from up high on the hill there, right down to my place on the beach. The cliffs are steep and there were different tracks that worked their way down—different generations of kids and lovers and pissed poets. Alistair had had quite a bit to drink and he had these new poems he had to show me. He filled a decanter of sherry that had a glass top in it—this was the amazing bit—and on his way down he lost his footing. Suddenly there was an almighty thump—it was night-time—and I thought, 'What's happened?' I came out and there's Alistair picking himself up. He had the decanter of sherry still full to the top with the glass thing in it and he had these new poems including 'Why Don't You Talk To Me?' and, I think I'd be right in saying, 'Blue Rain'—some lovely love poems and he'd just written a whole bunch of them.

He used to see a lot of my poems and he was never over-enthusiastic. If something was good, you knew he meant it if he said, 'Gosh, I like that.' He wasn't over-effusive with his praise, not at all. He was a very good editor—and highly literate, you know.

Meg was a great friend. At the time I met them, she may have written a few poems but she wasn't dedicated to it—it definitely came later for her. Her first volume took me by surprise, it was a bloody good book *A Durable Fire*, it's called. Meg wrote a different sort of poetry—it was more domestic. It wasn't meant to knock you out in the same sort of way—it worked in a different way. She wrote some lovely powerful poems but dear old Meg would often feel pushed out by the blokes. At times she could be very childish, quite petulant. Other times she was one of the wisest friends you'd ever have. She could be a very demanding friend. Sometimes she'd demand a lot and she didn't always get that with me. Like all friendships, it had its good times and not so good times, but overall it was a very important one.

Poem on Meg's Death

Your breathing, soft now,
silences the birds.
All I hear
is a tap dripping somewhere

I know is
your heart doing its
thing at
least for the moment.

I wait outside
while family attend.
They've no need to tell me
you're gone, Meg. The tap

stopped dripping, miraculously.
And the birds started
singing like there was
no tomorrow.

I toured with Alistair. I did two tours for the NZUSA Arts Council, the first in 1975 with Denis Glover, Hone Tuwhare and Alan Brunton, all of whom are dead. That was such a success that, four years later, the same Arts Council decided to do another one but this time using Hone, Alistair, Jan Kemp and myself. They were both bloody good tours but they were long. The first one was six weeks and the second—if my memory serves me right—was seven, eight weeks. I was used to living on the road but Alistair was not, and that tour was very hard on him. One time when we were in Masterton, Alistair was freaking out. Funnily enough, he's got a poem about Masterton called 'Small Town Blues' and he's got these lines:

...not three hours by road from my family,
and already I am homesick—
I am at best a poor traveller....

I miss the recognition of friends and family...

We were at the school—big school show—and we were all on stage and the hall was absolutely chocka with kids from all the schools brought in for the show. Alistair was up doing his stuff and there were kids down there talking among themselves. Alistair said, 'I've come here to read my poems to you. If you don't want to hear my poems, can you fuck off?' Most of the kids were awestruck that Alistair was there—it was just a few kids—I could see where it was coming from. But his outburst wasn't justified, it wasn't needed.

DENIS GLOVER

When the name Denis Glover is mentioned—and I'm guilty of this at times too—you start thinking of the colourful stories of the man, and what a Dickensian character he was, but right above, beyond and after and before all of that is the Denis Glover who gave us anthems of the land we live in. It's the old story—if the poet has a large personality, the media like to get into their unusual lifestyles, and none more so than Denis Glover, but beyond all of that we are left with the great poems. If I had never met him and didn't know him and his personality and all his charm and charge, it wouldn't make any difference. All I need to do is to go to the score.

I first met him when I was staying, many years ago, with my cousin by marriage, Jenifer, who was married to Allen Curnow. I was in my last year of school and I'd walked along the Waitakeres from Bethells, taking a few days on my own. I stayed at Anawhata a couple of nights then walked over to Piha and Karekare. Jenifer and Allen were vaguely expecting me and they were very generous—I was there for a night or two. This particular night, about midnight, a car pulled up on the road down below the house and Curnow, the great white chief, gave me the torch and said, 'Sam, would you go down and see who it is?' I heard these loud noises, 'Curnow! Curnow, you there?' and even at that stage I recognised that it was none other than Denis Glover. He'd arrived in Auckland—people didn't telephone each other in those days, they just arrived—expecting Curnow to be at home at Maunsell Road in Parnell and Curnow wasn't there. So he figured he'd be out at his bach at Karekare and jumped into a taxi with a couple of bottles of brandy to keep the party going and went all the way to the Waitakeres.

I also remember, when I was younger, going to the Auckland City Art Gallery where Denis Glover and Allen Curnow were doing a reading. As well as doing their own poems, Curnow was doing R. A. K. Mason's and Denis was doing Fairburn's. Looking back on it, it may have been one of the first literary events that I ever went to. Glover was just great, but I think he over-killed some of his poems a bit—sometimes he was a bit florid on it, in that old style. I shouldn't really say that because in a way it was the old style of doing things, like when he used to do Fairburn's 'The Rakehelly Man', he would give it the full drama.

I got to know Glover up in Paekakariki when he and Khura lived there, Khura being his lover. Mary was his wife, then in later years, long after they were separated and divorced, he lived with the crazy Khura, the marvellous Khura Skelton—old South Island stock, mad as a maggot and great. 'Glover' she'd say, 'where's my drink, Glover?' 'Get your own drink, you old bat.' The abuse between them was incredible. In the early days at Bottle Creek, there were lots of very good times, amazing times with Denis—always fuelled with incredible poems. There were all those other things he did—pugilist, printer and all those things—but right there at the heart of things for him, I know, were the poems. For him a poem was like the sanctuary lamp, the light was always there. It didn't matter how pissed or how cantankerous or how out of order he may have been, that sanctuary lamp was still burning. One of my favourite poems of Glover's is 'Superstition', a great poem. I remember saying it to him once and he wasn't all that pissed, but he just burst into tears that someone should know it.

Superstition

Look, I believe in signs, joss-sticks, flares,
Birds flying sinister or right,
A funeral passing, a cross-eyed man,
Spilt salt, a hairpin on the floor,
A horseshoe nailed the wrong way on the door.

Scared-scornful under ladders
I hopscotch pavement squares,
Spit on the dead bird and of course
Cross fingers for a white cat or horse.
On the month's day invoke rabbits or hares.

Portents and omens. Not superstitious I'll
Correct myself with a self-conscious smile.
Knowing each day is my day;
Yet thinking of my dear damned dead
Friends who sailed on a Friday.

[Denis Glover]

In my view Glover was the master of the refrain. He had a lovely touch, right through his poetry. Like all great poets he never wasted a word, and if there was an adjective there he would seriously question the use of it. Just as he had the perfect eye as a typographer, he had the perfect ear as a poet.

One of the hardest things he found as he got older was that he ran out of things to talk about. He hadn't dried up—he was doing those weekly poems on Wellington Harbour for the *Dominion* newspaper—but he would've given anything to recapture the magic of 'Sings Harry' or 'Arawata Bill' or 'The Magpies'. Having said that, towards the end he wrote one of his great poems, about himself and Khura. When he had something to talk about or sink his teeth into, he still had it, certainly.

I toured with Denis Glover and did different gigs with him. On the Student Arts Council tour with Hone Tuwhare and Alan Brunton—which was a nationwide tour of venues, night venues and high schools—Denis was amazing. He'd drink all day, every day and he was in a permanent state of something pretty bloody good. He could function most of the time—not all the time—and when he did function, he shone. He was usually the master of the occasion.

That tour, the Four Poets Tour, started in Whangarei, and it was a hard-working tour. I'd been on the road myself for at least a few years at this stage so I knew what touring was about. At the end of it, by the time we got to Invercargill, I was

With Denis Glover, c. 1970

pretty stuffed but Denis could have done the whole thing again. He had huge stamina. There was one time in Christchurch when Denis and I were going to a convent school for girls and we had to be there at nine o'clock in the morning. I got there on time, but there was no sign of Glover. I was into about the first quarter hour, holding forth, when Denis arrived at the back of the hall, pissed as a newt, arm-in-arm with a well-known old madam, who ran a well-known brothel in Christchurch. People could throw a lot of things at Denis because he offended a lot of people, but he was a gentleman. What's that line? 'He was a gentleman from sole to crown, clean favoured and imperially slim.' (From Edwin Arlington Robinson's poem 'Richard Cory'.)

On that particular tour I had my old ambulance, which Denis would call 'The Sambulance'. I bought it from Michael Smither, the painter, in about '75—once upon a time it had been the Roxburgh ambulance in Central Otago. It was a big yellow ambulance and, rather than travel with the group in their little minibus, Denis would quite often say to me (and Minstrel was travelling with me too), 'Any chance of joining you for the next leg?'

I saw quite a lot of Denis between '75 and his death in 1980. He'd been living in Paekakariki but by the time he went on tour in 1975 he was living in Wellington, on The Terrace. Not long before he died he was living in Strathmore—he used to refer to himself as 'The Earl of Strathmore'—but he missed the sea. He was only happy really, like myself, when he was in close cooee of the sea. When he had the fall which led to his being put in hospital, which led to his dying, it was actually during

Crossing a ford in what Denis Glover called the Sambulance

the move they were making—he and his lovely wife, Lynn—to Breaker Bay. Number 100 Breaker Bay was going to be their address. I took him over for a drive to have a look at it one day before they moved in. He was very frail then. Apparently he was trying to carry some box which he probably shouldn't have been trying to lift. He toppled and that was the start of the fall of the big kauri tree—not big in stature but bloody big in all those things that matter. The Welsh say you measure the man from the shoulders up.

A. R. D. FAIRBURN

We had a copy, when it first came out, of Fairburn's volume *Strange Rendezvous*. It included 'To a Friend in the Wilderness' addressed to Sir Douglas Robb, an Auckland surgeon who was a friend of theirs and very much part of the Fairburn brigade. A lot of Fairburn poems take place around Mahurangi on the East Coast north of Auckland. That was very much Fairburn country and 'To a Friend in the Wilderness'—if it's got a geographical setting—would have been set there: '…let it rip, let go the rope… Make life a long week-end…'

I go along with that—it's been a dictum of mine since I was very young. You talk about lost weekends but this is a long weekend. One of the first road songs I ever wrote was called 'War Mashes'—not sure if it was ever published—and the last line in it was 'Fairburn all to do with you', about hitting the road and taking your sleeping bag. He's certainly one of the reasons that I felt poems would be central to my way of life.

I don't think he wrote towards the end of his life as much as he would've liked. He had a lot of worries at the time—financial worries and a big family to support—and his own precarious way of disappearing sometimes. There's a story told of him going down to buy some chops and five days later he came home—without the chops. From what I've read and what people who knew him have told me, there was that feeling that the lyric fire had dimmed a bit—although he still wrote satirical things. I never heard him saying poems live, only on record that I can remember.

I've heard a lot of criticism, especially over the feminist years, of Fairburn and how he was a male chauvinist and didn't respect women. In my opinion he's written some of the most beautiful love poems that have ever been written in this country and some of the most humane and beautiful verse—things like 'Full Fathom Five' and 'The Cave', which is an extraordinary, primeval poem—although some of his poems do go on a bit long. 'The Dominion', the big poem that was to be his epic, I think someone described it as one of the greatest epics that ever failed.

The Cave

From the cliff-top it appeared a place of defeat,
the nest of an extinct bird, or the hole where the sea hoards its bones,
a pocket of night in the sun-faced rock,
sole emblem of mystery and death in that enormous noon.

We climbed down, and crossed over the sand,
and there were islands floating in the wind-whipped blue,
and clouds and islands trembling in your eyes,
and every footstep and every glance
was a fatality felt and unspoken, our way
rigid and glorious as the sun's path
unbroken as the genealogy of man.

And when we had passed beyond
into the secret place and were clasped
by the titanic shadows of the earth,
all was transfigured, all was redeemed,
so that we escaped from the days
that had hunted us like wolves, and from ourselves,
in the brief eternity of the flesh.

There should be the shapes of leaves and flowers
printed on the rock, and a blackening of the walls
from the flame on your mouth,
to be found by the lovers straying
from the picnic two worlds hence, to be found and known,
because the form of the dream is always the same,
and whatever dies or changes this will persist and recur,
will compel the means and the end, find consummation,
whether it be
silent in swansdown and darkness, or in grass moonshadow-mottled,
or in a murmuring cave of the sea.

We left, and returned to our lives:

the act entombed, its essence caught
for ever in the wind, and in the noise of waves,
for ever mixed
with lovers' breaths who by salt-water coasts
in the sea's beauty dwell.

[A. R. D. Fairburn]

Things might have been different for Fairburn if he'd been able to get a literary grant or a Burns Fellowship and take off for a year or two, although with a big family growing up it's not always that easy to take off to Dunedin. He was the one who wrote that beautiful four-liner called 'Note on a State Literary Fund' (1948):

Here is a piece of wisdom
I learnt at my mother's knee:
The mushroom grows in the open,
The toadstool under the tree.

So Fairburn suffered the bad rap or bad rep. Some people can't get past the fact that he wasn't the perfect male or something. Women found him attractive—I don't know if he was a womaniser, I didn't know him well enough for that, but he certainly liked women a lot and women liked him. The expression 'larger than life' has been used to describe him.

ROBIN HYDE

One poet I would love to have been able to talk to when I was a bit older, but who wasn't even around when I was born, was Robin Hyde. She died in 1939, the same day war was declared on Germany. The New Zealand High Commissioner in London, Bill Edge, was a friend of my father's. Bill gave the eulogy when Robin died—she committed suicide when she was thirty-four years old, very young—and he said at her funeral, which was obviously a very sad affair, 'even in this time of war when man fights man and nation fights nation, we must make time for our little poet.' If you read Robin Hyde's letters, there are a lot of letters to Bill Edge; he helped her in lots of ways.

One of the last volumes published after her death—in fact, I think my father had something to do with it; I know Bill Edge did because he was acknowledged—was called *Houses by the Sea*, which is such a great title. It's one of those archetypal titles, you think, 'How did anyone find that one?' It's such a beautiful book. One of my favourite poems is one she wrote about her mother, 'The People'—a phenomenal poem: 'How she grew old happened in fine-darned places...'

Robin Hyde is a poet who I revere, she's so good. I was strongly influenced by her. She had a few supporters, like John A. Lee and Bill Edge, but she had a hard life.

from *The People*

II

How she grew old happened in fine-darned places,
Cracked pictures, seen too close: you'd barely know …
She was a red-haired woman, two little lines
Sharp cut between her brows: her eyes looked tired
As long as I remember, and her strong mouth sad.
Still she held firmly: when we went for walks
It was I who flagged: you'd never guess what frocks
She made us, while the clean thread broke and broke,
And I stood pricking at red sateen, or spoke
Roughly: that dance, the only one we had,
I remember Judy's frock of petals, wired
Bright blue, with silver wrappings round the stalks.

Sometimes I loved her: but I liked smooth faces
Like the other mothers had, and told her so.
She laughed: she was never frightened: she took knocks
Square on the mouth, and wouldn't hit you back:
I never saw my mother dressed in black
But grief came … and she never let it go.

[Robin Hyde]

HONE TUWHARE

I remember when I first saw Hone perform; it was when Pete Seeger was here in 1962 as part of the build up to the protests about Vietnam. They did a show in Auckland at St Matthew-in-the-City. When *No Ordinary Sun* came out I saw him on television and he was introduced by an academic from the English Department, John Reid (J. C. Reid), who sort of championed Hone's poems.

I got to know Hone, as a lot of people did, and we became very good friends—we were very fond of each other. Quite a few of my own poems were addressed to him, like 'Hilary':

I too had a lean
Aunt. She died at thirty....

That's a reference to a poem of Hone's, which I'd always loved, one of the great, great, Tuwhare poems, 'Flood'.

Flood

In the back country
hard rain
is bucketing

Here
in the narrowing light
the river bellows
fatly

From high ground
I mark
twin rows of willow
dishevelled arms
clutching drunk roots
hoarding
bits of old bridge-planking
the body of a beast
puff-bellied
hind feet sticking out

I ask:
when will the waters clear
the eels breathe easy again?

Shall I be able to ford
the river soon: visit
a lean Aunt?

[Hone Tuwhare]

I said to Hone once, having heard him tell it, 'Who was your lean Aunt, Hone?' He said, 'I don't know, it may have been my mother.' I was interested in his reference to that 'lean Aunt'—such a great phrase.

On the verandah of Death's Corner, Pauatahanui. Jan Kemp, Alistair Campbell, Hone Tuwhare, Sam Hunt: Four New Zealand Poets Tour, 1979

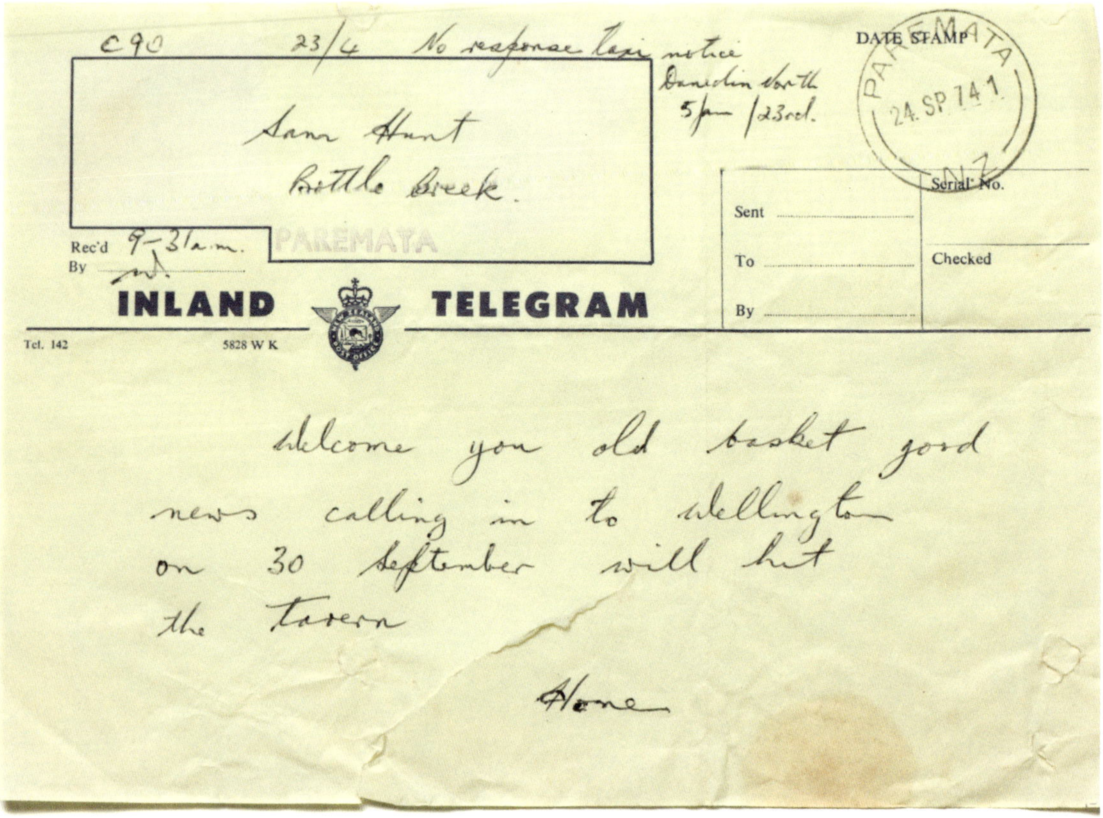

C90 23/4 No response tax notice Dunedin North 5pm /23rd.

DATE STAMP

PAREMATA 24 SP 74 1 N.Z.

Sam Hunt
Bottle Creek.

Rec'd 9-31a.m.
By

PAREMATA

Sent

To

By

Serial No.

Checked

INLAND TELEGRAM

Tel. 142 5828 W K

Welcome you old basket good news calling in to Wellington on 30 September will hit the tavern

Hone

The constellation of Tuwhare—poems of Hone's that one would never forget—one I have loved and loved and loved. Recently I was in Whangarei with Alf and we were in The Warehouse, and my bargain that day was a woman who came up to me and introduced herself and said, 'My mother is Hone's sister.' We were talking away and she said, 'One poem of Hone's that was special for us was "Tangi",' and I said it was one of my all-time favourites. There are so many!

Hone used to be terrible with microphones but he got better. It was a bit 'un-Maori' to use a microphone, although I always thought Prince Tui Teka did a pretty good job, and so did Billy T. Quite a few years later, in the '80s, Hone and I were both invited to do a performance at a Taranaki festival, a big venue. I hadn't seen Hone for a while, but up to that time he didn't like microphones and probably wouldn't use one, and people would miss his show completely because he wasn't using it. On this occasion, in New Plymouth, I actually said to the sound guy, 'Just watch Hone because he plays games, turns the microphone off and doesn't use it.' What I'd forgotten was that, in the few years since I'd seen Hone, he'd spent a lot of time in Germany and done a lot of public performance. Anyway, when it came time for the sound check Hone was right there at the microphone. Dalvanius would have been proud.

The last time I went to visit Hone, down at Kaka Point, I didn't see him; he was out for the day. I was with Eileen, touring, and had a couple of days off, and we stayed at a motel at Kaka Point. I don't like popping in on people but Hone didn't have a phone so we went round and the house was open. I thought maybe he was asleep. It was a pretty basic little place by the sea, the Pacific Ocean crashing in. We went into the house. I had a bottle of wine I wanted to leave, and a note, but then I looked into the bedroom and suddenly had a chill and thought 'Shit, he's dead.' Eileen didn't come inside; she felt quite spooked by the feeling. I looked to make sure, but the bed had been slept in. It was unmade but there was no Hone in it, so we left the note. It turned out he'd been out being photographed for the programme which eventually came out after his death, the setting of *Tuwhare* that Charlotte Yates did. She and another lady were staying at the same motel and I said, 'Charlotte, what are you here for?' She said she'd been filming with Hone all day. He got home and got my note, and was absolutely rapt and was hoping to see me, but we didn't because we had to leave very early the next morning, so I didn't see him and he died soon after.

He was a great friend, a lovely man. My mother got on very well with him. He loved coming to our place, my parents' place where I grew up. He often used to come to Milford Beach to visit when I was there. We would meet up at the Milford Marina or the Mon Desir and more often than not end up at our place afterwards. I remember Hone going out and serenading my mother on the front lawn. He was a great singer—sometimes he'd burst into a Frank Sinatra song—he had a beautiful voice.

GORDON CHALLIS

I would say coming across Gordon Challis's poems was one of the great moments of my life. There was a particular poem, a translation—I was to learn later that Gordon Challis had done quite a lot of translating of poems from Spanish—and the particular poem that bowled me over was by a Peruvian poet, César Vallejo. It's a sonnet called 'Black Stone on Top of a White Stone'.

Black Stone on Top of a White Stone

I shall die in Paris, in a rainstorm,
On a day I already remember.
I shall die in Paris – it does not bother me –
Doubtless on a Thursday, like today, in autumn.

It shall be a Thursday, because today, Thursday
As I put down these lines, I have set my shoulders

To the evil. Never like today have I turned,
And headed my whole journey to the ways where I am alone.

César Vallejo is dead. They struck him,
All of them, though he did nothing to them,
They hit him hard with a stick and hard also
With the end of a rope. Witnesses are: the Thursdays,
The shoulder bones, the loneliness, the rain, and the roads...

[César Vallejo]

Round about that time—in the early '60s—Gordon Challis's first volume of poems, *Building*, was published by Caxton Press. It's a collection of his own poems including some quite Spanish sort of poems, for example there was one called 'Elegy for Alfonso Dotti y Millett':

It's near at hand, his country,
and I went there yesterday
went to walk and listen
for a soothing sound and peace...

Gordon Challis was a discovery, and when I bought his book *Building*, I loved the title, being both a noun and a present participle. I loved a lot of his poems, like 'The Asbestos-suited Man in Hell', and one of my great favourites, 'The Iceman'. The last poem in the book is what in my opinion is one of the great love poems of all time, written to his first wife Magda, who was Spanish:

Poem for Magda

When I am fit to speak of love the words will come
as easily as wheat puts forth its ample grain
or sunlight skips bright stones across a river.
My tongue thus far is husked and makes harsh sound
and shall not sing until I hear the growth of grain,
until I hear your name in all things blessed forever.

When I am fit to speak of love you may be past
your crest of youthful movement and your grace of line.
It will be late to praise you, late to flatter
myself by implication, finder of your eyes.

And there will be no need to find new ways
to ask or tell each other what's the matter.

When I am fit to speak of love will be a day
of neither signs nor revelation. It might occur
some time when sleeping at my side I'll feel you cry
and wake to hands that make your dream not true,
some moment when you're ironing or touch your hair—
simple and warm as clothes fresh-folded on a chair.

[Gordon Challis]

It's a beautiful poem, and then he stopped, and then the poems stopped, and I always wondered what happened to him. There was a forty-year silence between *Building* and his next volume, which came out some years ago, called *The Other Side of the Brain*, published by Steele Roberts. I would love to know if he was writing, if he was keeping his hand in for those silent forty years. Talk about forty days and forty nights in the desert—this was forty years. Whether it was a desert I don't know; I've only spoken to Gordon Challis on the telephone, I've never met him. When his collection *The Other Side of the Brain* came out forty years on, I was a little bit hesitant actually, I was wondering whether he'd lost it in that time, but no, far from it. There's still this wonderful neurotic sort of craziness.

I will be buried deep
under a cattle stop...

So he's been a big presence for me. He's very under-anthologised—ignored, I guess, because he made a burst onto the literary front in the 1960s and then went silent for all those years. You read a little bit of yourself into a lot of other people's situations, particularly when it comes to drying up, feeling that you've not really got anything much to say. I'd love to see a good collected poems of Gordon Challis. I can't think of any poets who write the sort of poems that he writes, a very particular kind of poem, I don't quite know the word for it. He has a very distinctive voice, unmistakably his voice.

putting it on the page

I think of publishing as choosing to make something public—you publish something. When I was about sixteen I self-published *Between Islands*—this was a handmade book that I typed and bound myself, and I produced four copies—terrible poems (see pages 26/27). But after this I started to have poems published. I remember one of the first great joys of being published was when I had four poems I'd written over on Rangitoto Island, called *Rangitoto Cycle*, published in *The Northland Magazine*, which in those years—the early 1960s—came out of Kaikohe up here in the North. They gave me the centre spread, and I was just so chuffed. And around about that time I was published in a New Zealand edition of *Poetry Australia*, with many of my heroes—Baxter, Alistair Campbell, Vincent O'Sullivan, Fleur Adcock—as well as in *Landfall*.

The Bottle Press emerged when I was living at Bottle Creek in the late '60s. Meg Campbell's brother, Bob Andersen, was teaching at Wainuiomata College, and he had the idea to publish broadsheets, with poems and artwork, as he had access to a printing press at the College. Bob had some publishing experience through working with Alister Taylor, but he didn't know how to use the press. There was a fellow there who was a printer, however—had something to do with where the press had come from—and he taught us about compositing and the comp stick and we used to go over at weekends when the kids weren't there. The core of Bottle Press was Bob and his wife Honey, myself and Robin White.

Robin is the closest I've got to a sister. She's eight days younger than me. When I first met Robin, I was already living at Bottle Creek and I'd come up to a performance in Auckland put on at Auckland University. It was a very literary affair but it was well done, big audience. Afterwards there was the inevitable party and the inevitable lovely women, and one of the loveliest of them all was Robin. She was an Elam art student and we got on really well. After Elam she had to go teaching for a year to deal with her student bond. She'd been down to stay at Bottle Creek—in fact some of the earliest paintings that she did of Paremata were done on that first visit—and she struck on the idea of teaching down there, so she taught at Mana College. We weren't romantically involved and even if we had been, we were both crabs, both needed our own bit of mudflat, thank you. We were really good mates and I got her a cottage that belonged to Captain Crab, a great old Paremata figure, a retired sea captain. Marvellous name, Captain Crab—sounds like something out of SpongeBob Squarepants. He had quite a big property with numerous cottages on the estuary. I wrote a poem once called 'October in the Bay Part II' and it's about him. So Robin moved into the cottage, often painting right through the night, and teaching art at Mana College.

The Bottle Press started with a poem of mine, 'A Flat Fat Blues', and I think the second was another poem of mine called 'A Song About Her'. Robin had done the linocut of my house over in the macrocarpas, so we loaded up with lots of alcohol and whatever else was needed, and disappeared over to Wainuiomata and shacked up under the school for the whole weekend. The only problem was that we ran out of paper, and we only did seventy copies, which was a real limited edition; we'd normally do 700. It sounds awful, but it was a deep orange matt paper. It was good quality though, and we went to a lot of trouble setting the type, so we were justifiably proud of what we had once we had finished.

The following night I was going up to the Paekakariki pub with Robin, to meet friends, including Denis Glover and Khura Skelton, and we had a copy of 'A Song About Her' to give to Denis. Well, he looked at it and said, 'Robin, that's wonderful, that is wonderful. Sambo, this is one of the few good poems you have written. What a shame you've pied the font in an 'a' of "Makara".' We'd done it in 12 point sans serif Gill, but one of the 'a's was 12 point serif Baskerville. His old typographer's eye went straight to it—we couldn't believe it.

I was aware of other broadsheets at the time, for instance one of James K. Baxter's 'Lament for Barney Flanagan', that sold round pubs in Wellington when he first wrote the poem. There were broadsheets of other Baxter poems—'A Death Song for Mr Mouldybroke' and 'A Bucket of Blood for a Dollar'—so certainly with Baxter there was a tradition of broadsheets. Wai-te-ata Press at Victoria University used to put out some—very fine in terms of printing, and in terms of poetry—very small volumes. The broadsheet was good for me because my venues weren't the literary poetry readings—they were more often some bar somewhere where people threw jugs. A number of times in the early days we had broadsheets, and I remember a girlfriend of mine was very good at selling them. She'd have a big pile and sell them for twenty cents a throw. They cost us nothing to do and I think we drank all the profits. The Bottle Press—sort of appropriate really isn't it?

In 1998–99 they had actually had a whole exhibition on Bottle Creek at the Porirua Museum of Arts and Cultures, which Helen Kedgley curated, and when it was opened they got us all together.

In the late '60s I met Alister Taylor, not to be confused with Alistair Campbell.

1.

Pith where a hard heart should be,
Climb but never hope to find
Anything but blossoms for a mind.
I'm more a lily than a tree.

And ignore the picture please.
I'm not what it makes out I am.
Just rip it up and call me Sam,
an old flat-footed cabbage tree

2.

Few believe in what they see.
Your friends prefer to call it myth
Passed down by drunken word of mouth:
They say such things can't be

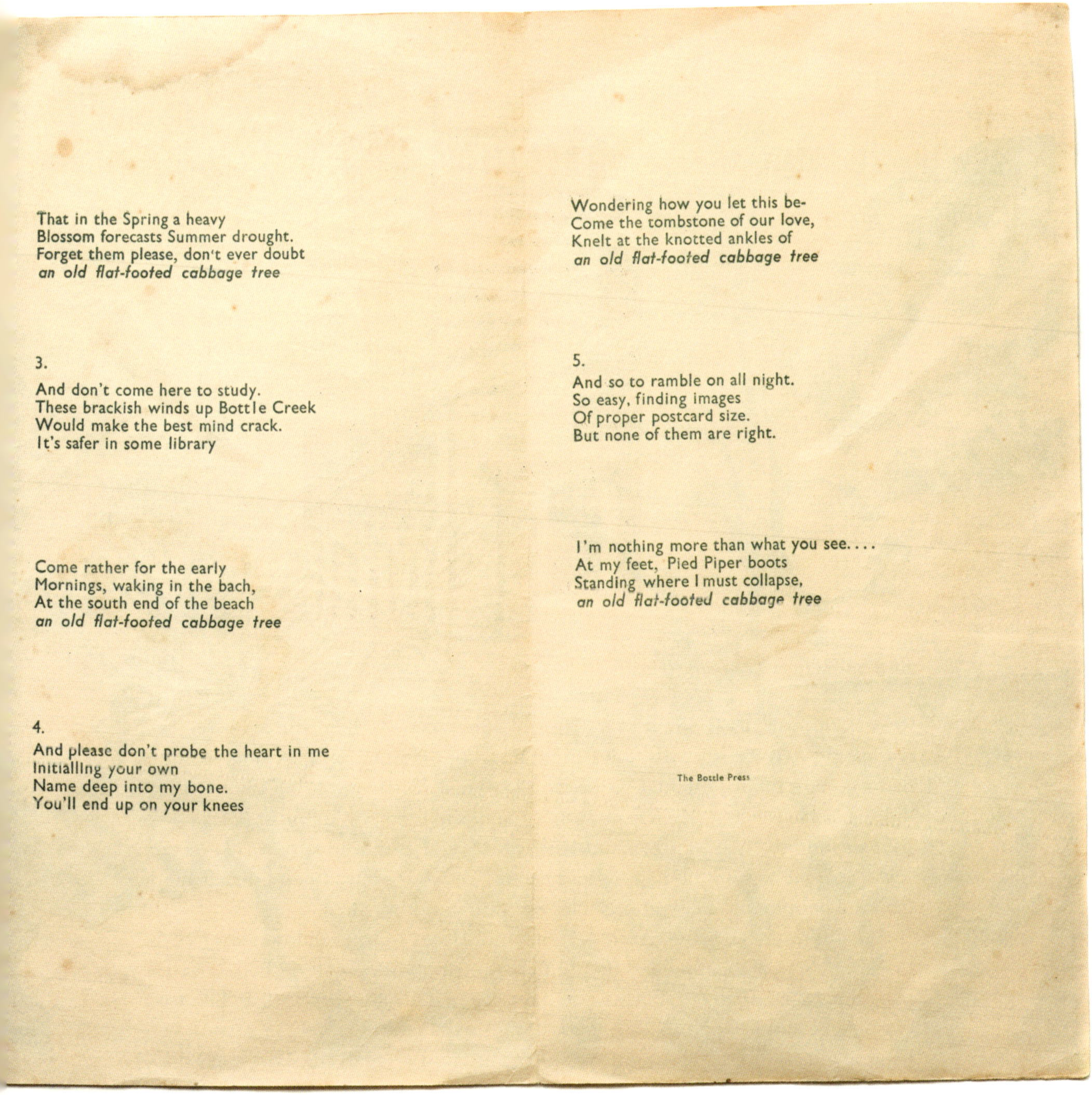

That in the Spring a heavy
Blossom forecasts Summer drought.
Forget them please, don't ever doubt
an old flat-footed cabbage tree

3.

And don't come here to study.
These brackish winds up Bottle Creek
Would make the best mind crack.
It's safer in some library

Come rather for the early
Mornings, waking in the bach,
At the south end of the beach
an old flat-footed cabbage tree

4.

And please don't probe the heart in me
Initialling your own
Name deep into my bone.
You'll end up on your knees

Wondering how you let this be-
Come the tombstone of our love,
Knelt at the knotted ankles of
an old flat-footed cabbage tree

5.

And so to ramble on all night.
So easy, finding images
Of proper postcard size.
But none of them are right.

I'm nothing more than what you see....
At my feet, Pied Piper boots
Standing where I must collapse,
an old flat-footed cabbage tree

The Bottle Press

Postcard of a cabbage tree – *an early broadsheet from The Bottle Press*

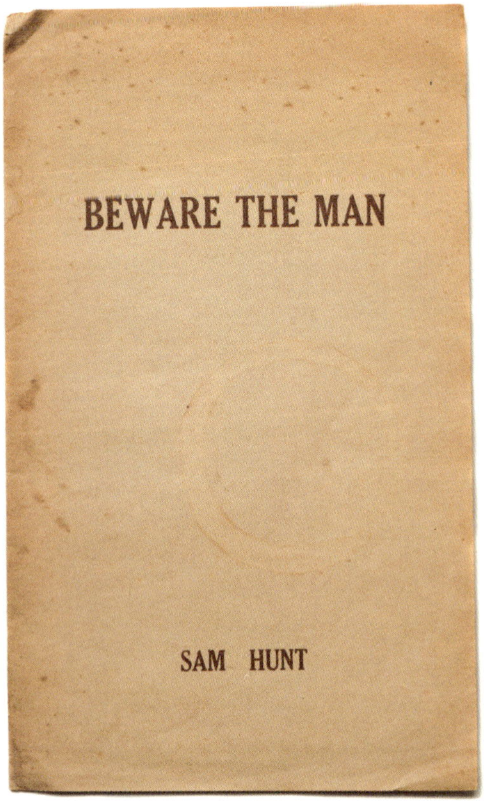

Broadsheets from The Bottle Press

Rupert Alister Halls Taylor, RAT for short. In fact, that was the name of his record company—Red Rat Records. I did an album with Mammal with his label. Alister had a certain rat-like quality—a survivor, I suppose, although I don't know if he did survive in the end. He was publishing books like Tim Shadbolt's *Bullshit and Jellybeans* and the first New Zealand *Whole Earth* catalogue, and later *The Little Red Schoolbook.* He was a bloody good publisher—or would have been good if he'd paid the people who made it possible. But that's another story.

I met him through Bob Andersen; he and Alister went to Palmerston North Boys High School together and they both became publishers. Alister had started a magazine called *Affair 69*—that's where I interviewed Alistair Campbell and R. A. K. Mason and other people. R. A. K. Mason was totally beyond access to anyone but he gave me an interview. Albion Wright of Pegasus Press talked of the early days of Denis Glover and things like that. Alister's day job was working for A. H. & A. W. Reed, and he was also working for National Radio, then called the YAs, He was a happening thing, old Alister, ready to take anyone on. When he was working for

Reed he accepted a manuscript of poems of mine called *From Bottle Creek*. There were delays and people were dicking around, and in the meantime Alister had left Reed and set up his own publishing house. He wanted to publish *From Bottle Creek* but he wanted to delay it a bit.

By then I'd written another book of poems called *Bracken Country*, a slim book. He published it in 1971, not as Alister Taylor but as Glenbervie Press—he lived in Glenbervie Terrace at the time. It was a very simple, very elegant little book—just a very limited edition. I've always been a bit anti these limited editions—I think it's a bit pretentious, assuming the value before you've actually been out in the market. I like something that becomes valuable because it's sought after.

In 1972 I did my second book with him, by this time as Alister Taylor Publishers, and that was *From Bottle Creek*. It had a glossy silver cover that somebody rather

Bracken Country,
Glenbervie Press, 1971

meanly described it as an elephant-sized pack of Silver-Tex condoms. *From Bottle Creek* caused great upset in the literary world—well not the literary world but the booky world—because it became a bestseller. The book was actually four small volumes inside the silver cover, with the poems handwritten out. It wasn't even my handwriting but it cut through a few electric fences and in a funny way it helped to take the poems a little more down off the bookshelf than they had before.

From Bottle Creek was certainly considered our greatest success in terms of publishing poetry. When it came out, 'Kaleidoscope', the Sunday evening television arts programme, did a full-hour documentary about me. The next day I got the train down to Porirua to do some shopping or whatever and decided that it was quicker to hitch-hike back than wait for the next unit. The first car that came along stopped and there were a couple of blokes—farmers—going back up into the Rangitikei. They picked me up said, 'Where are you going?' I said, 'Just a few

The cover and the four volumes of From Bottle Creek, *Alister Taylor, 1972*

miles up the road to Paremata, please.' He said, 'I know your voice, you're not the poet I heard on television last night are you?' So overnight, I had a profile.

Alister and I went on to publish a few more books—in 1973, *South into Winter: Poems and Roadsongs*; and in 1975, *Time to Ride*. *South Into Winter* was an interesting one. Alister always loved his colours, and he used a bright purple card for the outside cover. I remember that I happened to be in Nelson at the time the book was released. Well as they say, sunny bloody Nelson—Bob Anderson from the ABC Bookshop gave me a wonderful big window display to mark the occasion, but with the sun shining by eleven o'clock you couldn't see anything on the covers—they had all faded beyond recognition.

Just after Tom was born, in 1976, for the first time in my life I had financial cares. I was suddenly landed with the idea of having a lady and a baby dependent upon me. I'd done quite a lot of work for Alister apart from just being the author

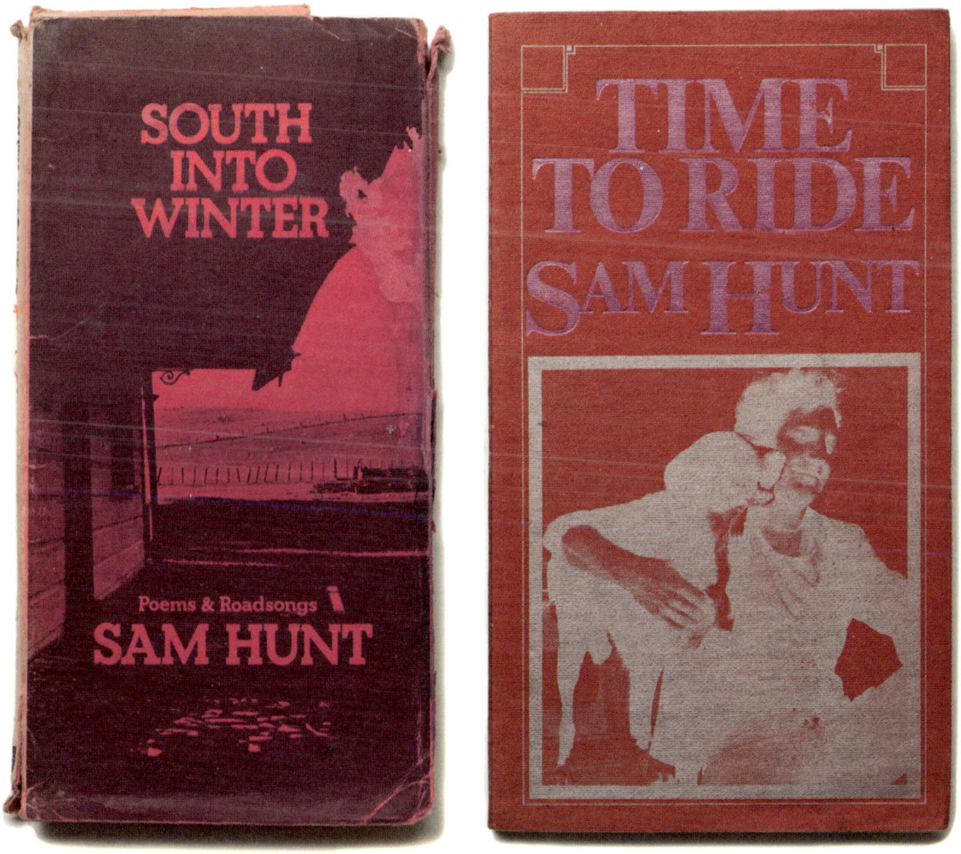

South into Winter, *Alister Taylor, 1973;* Time to Ride, *Alister Taylor, 1975*

of some books. I'd done a lot of truck driving for him, done a lot of editing for him, a lot of reading of manuscripts for him—I did all sorts of jobs for him. In fact, that's where I learned about proofreading. One of the later jobs I did—and Kristin was also involved in this job—was research on a book Alister Taylor published by John A. Lee called *Early Days in New Zealand.* I'd put a lot of work into it and at a particular point in my life when I needed money—for paying the rent, which by this stage wasn't two and six a week—I wasn't getting paid and he owed me $1500. The money never came through and I owed the store money which I didn't want to owe them—I don't like owing people money. Pauatahanui in those days was a real little country town, and here were these people I felt I was letting down.

Anyway, around about that time in my touring life I'd met a few heavies and one of them became a good friend. His name—good name—was Skin. He knew the story and he said, 'What we'll do, Sam, you and me'll get in the ambulance and go over to Martinborough.' So Minstrel, Skin and I went across and we drove through Martinborough, around the square—my memory of this is like a Tarantino movie!—where Alister's new red Mercedes Benz was. So we quietly ducked out a side road and down his road and parked across the cattle-stop at the top of the driveway. Sure enough, ten minutes later a swirl of dust—the red Mercedes—comes down the road. There's a big yellow ambulance parked across the cattle-stop and Taylor gets out and says, 'Get that bloody ambulance out of my way.' I said, 'Cheque book, Alister, money, $1500,' and walked over. Skin stayed in the passenger seat. Alister said, 'I haven't got it. Come round to the house, I'll drive down,' but we knew that once he'd gone down then we would have lost him. Sure enough, the cheque book was sitting on the dashboard, and before he saw it I reached and said, 'Here's your cheque book, Alister. You owe me $1500 plus travel. Cash.' I think we made it $1600. That was the end of my publishing with him. It was a shame, as he was such a good publisher.

I've often thought that if Alister hadn't come along to publish me then I don't know who would have—despite the financial differences, he provided terrific support and hospitality and he knew how to look after people. It was a timely match because I was starting to go out onto the stage more and more, and if I'd had to deal with some old tried and true left-over from the forties then I mightn't have been so happy. In terms of style and quality, and his ideas for what a book could do, he was way ahead of his time, a complete turn-around when you look at what the other publishers of his era were doing. So while there are aspects of the whole Taylor saga that leave me sad, there are an awful lot of fine memories.

When I decided to publish my next book, called *Drunkard's Garden,* I'd just moved to Death's Corner from Battle Hill. Chris Hampson and I published the book—did the whole thing; the first print was 4000 softback, 1000 hardback. I didn't have contracts with Taylor but I didn't want to bring a book out and then suddenly find embargoes put on it so I couldn't sell it, so I went to see my lawyer

Hugh Rennie and he got interested in the whole question of copyright. He checked all the background in terms of royalties not being paid, contracts not being signed or if they had been signed not being fulfilled by the publisher, and gave me the clearance to go ahead. Subsequently *Drunkard's Garden* was published—it was great fun—enormous fun.

The book was quickly reprinted, thanks to the publicity over the weekend of St Patrick's Day, 1977. This came about thanks to Dougal Stevenson who was the television newsreader of the day. We had a big party to launch *Drunkard's Garden* and Dougal and his wife Caroline were invited to the party, along with a few hundred other people—it went on for forty-eight hours, which was kind of appropriate for the book. Dougal was driving over from his home in Paremata to read the news at Avalon, and on his way over he called in to the party for a few hours. When he got over to Avalon he told the newsroom that there said there was a bloody good story over at Death's Corner, so the next thing we had a film crew over filming the party. It went out on television the next night as I recall and the next Monday the orders flooded in—I remember driving my old ambulance around absolutely chokka with parcels of books going off to bookshops around New Zealand.

Drunkard's Garden, *Hampson Hunt, 1978*

minstrel

In 1972, about the time I published my book *From Bottle Creek*, an old friend of mine, Keith Fox, died. This young, very healthy man—he was in his forties—was a wonderful person and a huge inspiration to me. He didn't write poems—it wasn't that direct—but it was direct in the sense of his belief in what I was doing. Anyway, when he was dying he put his hands on my shoulders—he didn't have much strength left in his hands—and said to me, 'You're the Minstrel', and as a bit of an afterthought—he always knew I liked dogs, he had a dog—he said, 'If you get a dog, maybe you should call it Minstrel.'

About three days later I was in my boatshed at Bottle Creek in the middle of a boozy afternoon with some friends when this very fine six-month-old, good-eyed and strong-eyed short-haired border collie came in. This beautiful dog just wandered in like he knew the way there. I think it was either that day or the next day or the day after that he became known as Minstrel.

The first testing time was walking over the Paremata Bridge, which was in those days—it was still Highway 1—a pretty dodgy place to walk with a dog. We were walking on that very narrow footpath and here was this young pup, only six months old—he'd only known me for six hours. I told him to stay behind me as we walked along the path over the bridge but he stepped down onto the busy road. I didn't just pick him up and put him back on the footpath, I picked him up and I threw him—not in anger—over the rail and he dropped about twelve feet to the water below. I trundled along and went over the fence and down the bank and he came running over the beach shaking himself. I tell you what, after that I never needed a lead on that dog.

Minstrel was a wonderful dog. He taught me something—well he taught me lots of things—but one thing he certainly taught me was that if you weren't comfortable in a situation you got out. If he didn't like the feel of a place—and he could tell a bad motel from a kilometre out of town before we got there—he'd just get uptight and, sure enough, we'd get to the motel and there'd be some uptight motelier who'd say, 'Ooo, we're not sure about dogs.' Minstrel was made a member of the Great Western motel chain. They had these plastic cards so you could get a ten per cent discount each time you stayed in one of their motels. I had my card, S. Hunt, and Minstrel had his own card with M. Hunt.

Minstrel certainly inspired a few poems—arguably wrote a few. Of course a dog—and this has been said before by people who have owned dogs—they teach you to look again. If you're going to write poems, one of the best things to do is to look again, take another look, pause, put yourself on pause. Dogs do actually put you on pause—you go for a walk with a dog and they're looking for something, sniffing around. They're on the case, which is a very similar process to writing a poem.

Before I met Minstrel I got to know Ken Gray—a local farmer who lived across on the other side of the estuary, ex-All Black—and his wife, Joy. He'd refused to play for the All Blacks in South Africa in about 1968, same time as Robin [White] moved down to live in Bottle Creek. I remember writing a poem called 'Robin at Midnight'—it's about visiting friends you miss—and that was Ken talking about being rejected from the All Blacks because he refused to play. He was one of the finest forwards they'd ever had, arguably the best in the history of the game. Anyway, as a farmer he knew a good sheepdog and when he saw Minstrel, Ken said, 'He's no stray, he's strong-eyed, he's a heading dog. He's fallen off a truck, I'd say. We'd better advertise.' Saturday morning *Dominion*, an ad went in—'Found, one strong-eyed sheepdog, six months, male' phone number, etc. Nothing came of it and years went by, and by the time Tom was born Minstrel was about seven and was looking after me on a full-time basis.

One Guy Fawkes night Joy and Ken invited Kristin, Tom—he was about eighteen months old—and me around. They were having a big fire—anything to do with Ken Gray had to be big and this was a massive bonfire. He didn't know how to do things on a small scale. Their place was in the Kakaho Valley going up to Mount Welcome, overlooking Kapiti Island. There'd been a big rugby match in Wellington that day and a lot of the All Blacks he'd lost contact with because of his political stance—like Colin Meads and Brian Lochore—they were there and they decided, I think, to bury the hatchet.

Not long before that there'd been on TV a series on the sheepdog trials. A dog from the Wairarapa—Mount Bruce—called King, cleaned up—100 out of 100, all the sheep in the pens with about ten seconds to spare. People said to me—including old Mrs Welden at the Pauatahanui store—'Did you watch that sheepdog trial programme on TV last night, Sam? That dog looked so much like Minstrel.'

Anyway, at Ken's party, I think it was Brian Lochore who said, 'What's King

Sam Hunt and Minstrel, mid-1980s

Hey, Minstrel

I know you're there.
I can hear you listening.

            Parked, say,
between a highway and river—
the roadbuilders left space
for dogs, and people like us.
The odd driver toots, spots
a man without a dog.
That's okay, you had to
die when you did.
We chose the day.
The day chose us.
It wasn't till after we buried you
there was any fuss.
Then it was Christmas.
I called up an old mate and
gave up the piss.

I know you're there.
You came by last night
just as I was talking to
a woman with the moon in her hair.

Nothing unusual in that. The moon's
been hanging around
an awful lot lately.
But you were there for sure.
She kept asking if I was all right
and kept repeating her name
as if I didn't know her.

Strange, the times since you died.
But while there's space
for dogs and people, a place
a man can park his car
between a highway, say,
and a river;

            or, more simply,
touch the moon, that's okay too.

doing here? That's got to be King!' All the bits and pieces started coming together. It turned out some Wairarapa shepherd owned King and that what Ken Gray had said all those years ago when he first met Minstrel—that he'd fallen off a truck, he'd been in training—was exactly what had happened. There had been two males—King and Minstrel—from the same litter so King was Minstrel's twin brother—Minstrel meets the King.

Minstrel obviously was as bright as his twin brother, who brought his intelligence to bear on living a very different life. I was touring pretty much all the time during those years, often doing school shows during the day and gigs at night, sometimes having breaks between tours. Minstrel had an instinctive sense of knowing where he was going to be welcome. If it was an uptight sort of situation, like at some schools, he'd know before we even drove through the gates. He'd just be hunkering down and you could see he wasn't going to get out and meet the kids when he was like that. At other schools—I remember Long Bay College was always a very welcoming school—he'd be out the window before I even asked whether he wanted to jump out and would come into the show and always behave himself.

My mother, who was quite nervous of dogs, used to say of Minstrel, 'He's an absolute gentleman.' He was a great dog—great company. I think we worked out he was just about seventeen when he died. When he was ready to die I rang my friend Pat Murphy, a local farm vet I met through Ken Gray—he was like the royal vet, 'vet to the corgies'. Pat was a great friend of Minstrel's—he loved Minstrel. He'd tell me in the early days what to feed him: 'Give him gravy beef and bones—don't worry about biscuits. These dogs just want meat and bones'—and that's what he had.

I remember ringing Pat this particular morning from the boathouse. Minstrel was very old and arthritic at this stage and going blind—those header dogs get glaucoma—and to my surprise, when the vet knocked on the door of the boathouse to come and do the deed—give him the injection—it wasn't Pat, it was a very nice woman vet. You always fear this day—how you'll handle it—but it all made sense at the time—it often does. The dog is ready to go. Later that day Pat came round and it turned out that this hardened farm vet had called his young assistant because he just couldn't deal with it.

The only thing I like about Roger Douglas is that he was expelled from the Labour Party on the same day that Minstrel died, but Minstrel's death got more coverage than Roger Douglas's sacking from the Labour Party. If I ever run into Roger Douglas, every time we get the same story: he'll tell whoever's there, 'The day they booted me out of the Labour Party was the day his dog died. TV1, TV3: leading item Minstrel Hunt's death; second thing, Minister of Finance sacked from the party. We both hit the six o'clock news and the late news.' Minstrel had a big following—every newspaper in the country covered his death. I had to make

At Battle Hill Creek, c.1976—Minstrel clearing the fence

myself unavailable for comment because it was getting ridiculous. Actually Brian Sweeney, my manager at the time, sent out a press release that covered it.

I buried Minstrel right above the boathouse, above the sand track, and planted a cabbage tree there, which is now a really big healthy cabbage tree—never got hit by all those things that cabbage trees get hit by. I've had dogs since then—just two. One was a long-haired border collie called Spark. He belonged to Jill Magan, Ian Magan's wife—Ian being an old friend, one of the people who founded Radio Hauraki. Jill died of cancer and I adopted Spark. That went well and then he got to the point of arthritis when I was on Waiheke Island. After that I had a beautiful dog, a working dog whose name was Mate. He lived high in the Rangitikei—belonged to a friend of mine—Rob Newcombe. I wrote the poem 'Rangitikei River Song' for Rob.

Rangitikei River Song

A man can only
find himself when lost.
Such country, this,
where all men are lonely:
plateau, hawk and rivermist:

country where a man at last
might lose himself, an end of talk;
find that gaunt-faced other
man who stalks these ridges:
plateau, rivermist and hawk:

no longer keeping eye
for crumbling edges,
lovers or the weather.
Listening, rather to the river:
hawk and high plateau,
rivermist below.

I met Rob through Ken Gray. Lovely man, Rob, very gentle, very good farmer. He did most of his farming on horseback and Mate was his heading dog. I was there on the eve of his death up in Rewa, high in the Rangitikei, looking right down on the river, and we were talking—he was very frail. Everything was looked after—the farm had been leased out; his son would eventually take over—and I said to him, 'Have you got homes for all the dogs, Rob?' 'Well, Mate's the problem,' he said. I knew that heading dogs are the least likely to transfer allegiance. The old huntaways, someone can get them to follow their basic commands but the heading dog is the prima donna. They often won't work for someone else—they get confused by different whistles and different commands, especially a dog of that age. So I said to Rob, 'Why don't I take him? I'll look after him,' and he said, 'Would you?' I said, 'Of course I would, I'd love to.' Well Rob died about two o'clock the following morning and Vanessa, his daughter, who had witnessed all this, said, 'I think Dad knew that once Mate was looked after, then everything was okay and he could just relax and die.' They had a very close bond, those two.

Mate was a cracker from the start. A few days later I came back for the funeral and I went to see him out with the other working dogs, out in his kennel. I knew I couldn't bring him back then because I was touring, but I just wanted to say 'Gidday, Mate' and take him for a drive. I had a Jaguar at that time and I always remember this very funny moment. I'd got a nice soft sack for the back seat—the leather seats in the Jaguar were very slippery for a dog—and I opened the back door and said, 'In you hop.' He looked round and he jumped up on the back of the boot—he was so used to going on the back of the ute—and of course he was slipping all around. I said, 'No, no, no, get down, you're coming with me.' Once he was in the back seat with the window wound down, I could see him thinking, 'Ahh, this is good!'

A week or two later Tom and his girlfriend picked him up from the farm. They stopped somewhere—top of the Desert Road, Turangi or somewhere—for a pie. Mate was in the back seat and Tom was sitting in the front with his pie in his hand and suddenly—poof!—it was gone. From the back seat, it was gone! Tom didn't feel it go. When you're competing with a whole lot of other dogs and the bone goes in, you don't look round and say, 'Can I have it?' Mate just went straight in and he had a look of complete innocence, apparently, and a bit of gravy was dripping down the side of his face—the telltale sign. He was very quick. He had been a working dog and brought his farm habits with him. You can take the dog off the farm but you can't take the farm off the dog. Minstrel had been brought up with more human manners. Mum would say Mate was more your working-class dog.

Mate also died of old age. One day I was over at the vet at Ruawai and I said to him—a good fellow—'What sort of vision would Mate have?' He said, 'I was hoping you weren't going to ask me—he's got none.' He was starting to walk into things and he was deaf too—he wasn't hearing commands—he was an old dog.

Here's a poem I wrote recently on the subject of dogs.

Chord (10)

When you get God's
attention, you just somehow
know it.
        And try as you do
not to, you can't help show it.

When a man pats a dog
the world is that
much better a place. The dog
wags its tail.
        Which must mean
something, to God; and the dogs.

music

Like poetry, there was a lot of music in my childhood. My father's family was deeply steeped in music—his father and his brother were professional musicians, both pianists. When I was growing up and writing early poems, and I was interested in words, along came great lines like:

> you can knock me down,
> step on my face…
> steal my car,
> drink my liquor from an old fruit jar
> but don't you
> step on my blue suede shoes

I thought, this is poetry, of a kind very different from that put forward at school—this was poetry in action.

Even with the combination of the recordings my mother and I listened to, the classical music, the Chuck Berry and Hank Williams lyrics, and writing my poems, I don't remember ever having the thought that I could possibly work with musicians.

However the Victoria University Students' Association used to have big Friday night bashes and they'd invited me to do some poems. I used to share the bill with the band Mammal, the line-up with Rick Bryant, Bill Lake, Rob Taylor, Tony Backhouse and Mike Fullerton. Once when we were doing a change-over—they'd been playing and then it was my turn—Mike Fullerton and Rob Taylor stayed on stage, hanging round just quietly, and I think Mike started tapping along to a poem. He started to shuffle off at the end of it and I said, 'You stay there, you've got yourself a job.'

So we started going on tour together quite a bit. It would be 'Presenting Mammal with Sam Hunt'. There were other bands involved in this touring too, like

TAMBURLAINE BLERTA
MAMMAL SAM HUNT
$1.$1·20
MASTERTON TOWN HALL 21 JULY 8P.M. BOOKINGS FARMERS
PALMERSTON NORTH OPERA HOUSE 22ND JULY 8P.M. BOOKINGS: COLLINSON & CUNNINGHAMME
DOME PROMOTIONS

One of the last shows at the Gluepot Tavern, Auckland, 1988

Blerta and Tamburlaine with Simon Morris, which was more acoustic. Mammal was heavy rock, which has always been my tipple rather than the more folky music. We performed together—Mammal and myself—at the very first rock music festival they ever had in New Zealand—The Great Ngaruawahia Music Festival in 1973. At a certain point along came Alister Taylor—he'd already published some of my poems, and he suggested we make a record for his label, which would include just straight poems told by me, tracks done by Mammal of my poems with me not there, and also tracks where I was also involved in the vocals, like 'Sandshoe Shuffle'—Rick Bryant does the verses and I do the choruses and we swap round at the end. It was good. We used Alex Lindsay's string quartet, and a composer, Ian McDonald, produced it. Rick had a lot to do with it too, behind the scenes.

We recorded it in the old Broadcasting House building on Bowen Street. Its title was *Beware the Man.*

I loved the experience and since then, over the years, I've worked with many musicians. I worked first with the Warratahs in Upper Hutt, many years ago. It was a great night, and a good friendship developed with the band, especially Barry Saunders and Sid Limbert. These have been two of my best friendships to have come from working on the road. I love the Warratahs' music. It's great being backstage when you hear them go on. First there is silence, and then suddenly this great ship is underway—they have a big sound when they get going, and they really know how to go for it. We've worked together collaboratively as well, and the way it has developed is that they will have a song, like 'Cape Turnagain', and I will bring in a poem that accompanies it at the end of the song, in this case a poem called 'Naming the Gods', with them backing me. We feel it works really well together.

I've worked a lot with Hammond Gamble, who is another dear friend made on the road—I love his music, his guitar playing. I think Gary McCormick may have introduced us, and the three of us toured a lot with Gary organising these tours. And I've worked with Split Enz too, on an ENZSO tour in Australia, when Eddie Rayner orchestrated the songs and they got various guests involved. Our band was the Adelaide Symphony Orchestra—110 strong. Honestly, sometimes you'd be out there on the edge of the stage giving it to the audience and you'd feel you were going to be physically blasted off the stage by this incredible sound.

A gig in the late 1970s

Dave Dobbyn and Annie Crummer were also there on that tour, and we had a great time.

I remember going out at the Sydney Entertainment Centre (maybe 15,000 people out there), and the last track before half-time was 'Under the Wheel'. The orchestra's going and Peter Scholes was the guest conductor—a great man to work with. Came my moment and I couldn't remember my opening lyric. I had no prompt but I knew my moment—when the harpist came in and the conductor would turn round and point his baton in my direction. I had to do something so I did a poem, not by Phil Judd or Tim Finn but by W. H. Auden: 'Lady, weeping at the crossroads, would you meet your love in the twilight…'

I did it completely to the right timing and most people would never even have noticed. I came off stage and Tim Finn said, 'What was that? That was great!' Even the conductor hadn't noticed because they're not listening to the words, so no one picked it up. Fortunately we've got it on tape, and it sounds great with the Adelaide Symphony Orchestra playing backing to this very strange poem of Auden's.

I've always felt very comfortable in the music world. I can say without any need to amplify it that I far, far, far prefer the company of musicians and the work they do than the literary crowd. I can't stand the literary environment. The musicians have a sense of performance, however plunky-plunk they may be, they have a sense of occasion—it's performance time, and they are not out the front having a drink with the punters, but backstage pacing up and down. And the whole energy that builds up and releases itself in a performance is very much what I am about, rather than sitting around listening to questions and answers. I've always called this the 'CH3 factor'—the Charm, Charge and Chant factor. If it don't have those three elements then I'm not interested.

I've also always had a strong affinity with songwriters and I believe it's largely to do with the fact that their idea of poetry is

Performing at the Great Ngaruawahia Music Festival, 1973

On the road, a motel room somewhere

quite similar to mine. It's got to sound okay before it does anything else. The questions for me are can you hear it, does it have a voice? Sometimes it mightn't be a particular key or voice you're hearing but maybe just a rhythm that's got you going. I've had a wonderful time recently making an album with David Kilgour called *Falling Debris*. One of the remarkable discoveries for me in this process of working with David is that he brought his music to my poems or lyrics that already existed. Sometimes there were lyrics that I supplied where he needed them, but in most cases they already existed. What I found remarkable was that, in pretty much every case of any poem that I remember the genesis of—that first conscious awareness that something's going on there—that's exactly what he homed in on. For example, on *Falling Debris* there's a song called 'I Throw You Flowers'. I know that the first words written down, and certainly the first to come to me, were 'because you do, you always do', and that's exactly where he came in. He didn't know that, I didn't highlight that part and say that's where it started from.

Same thing happened with 'Every Time it Rains Like This', although that one was probably more obvious because it's got a stated refrain. I think it's because he and I have such similar ways of working that he instinctively recognised the first half-beat of the poem's life—the poem's jugular. He was onto it, in a way that you can only do instinctively. I was staggered by that; I hadn't had that experience before. There was another track called 'Talking of the Weather', and when David sent me the first demo of that I thought it was simply the sung version of it—that's how it's meant to be sung.

Every Time it Rains Like This

Every time it rains like this:
rain from early morning falling
thick with light: the whole
wide world of our bay
has given in: rain: and nothing any
friend or fisherman can do

Every time it rains like this:
oilskins sweat in boatsheds:
well indoors: all's gone on for
far too long… I am
one with rain, no longer to
that woman there; we're through

Every time it rains like this:
I walk hangover beaches, make
no more sense of it:
in love with a winter woman,
a woman when she steams, I kiss
wet winter lips, return to you

Every time it rains like this

I often describe my poems—slightly tongue in cheek but also seriously—as poems for the tone deaf. Well David has taken them beyond that and made them into something else—poems for the highly tuned. I've loved working with him. I don't know how the album will go, I don't know what people will think of it. I won't say I don't care because I do care, but mostly I care for the songs he's made, and I'm pleased for the whole process—it's felt natural, not forced, not like we're trying to prove anything.

I was invited to be Leonard Cohen's 'special guest' last year—another name for support act but it just makes you feel better. I got well paid for it too. They often don't pay support acts very well but they paid me very well and I know who made sure of that: Leonard Cohen. Doing two opening shows for Leonard was a great privilege—like meeting a brother, that's what he said to me, like I've known you for years. The first show we did in New Zealand was in Wellington, and before I went on stage we were briefly introduced to each other—and to Sharon Robinson and the other people who became comrades over the next little while—then I went on stage and did my half-hour. When I came off stage there were a couple of stage crew with torches so I wouldn't fall over—it was dark after the stage lights—and somebody took me by the wrist as my eyes were still adjusting—almost like a mixture of leading me and feeling my pulse. As my eyes adjusted I realised it was Leonard with his fedora hat on and he said to me, 'That's poetry', and it was just lovely. He didn't say, 'That's poetry, man!' but just 'That's poetry' and led me out across to his dressing room where we consumed a few glasses of wine.

Musicians like David Kilgour, Barry Saunders, Bic Runga, my dear old friend Shona Laing, they take it out there and deliver it, follow my old maxim of 'tell the story, tell it true, charm it crazy'. That's what Leonard does every night to very big audiences, and for a lot of people it's quite a religious experience. He works from the stage and the page—I mean his poems work. You can get strength off the page as with any good poet, and there are things you get from the stage that you don't get from the page and vice versa. I think his recent collection of poems, *Book of Longing*, is one of the most beautiful books of poetry I own. And to go to a concert or get an album like *I'm Your Man* and the song 'Tower of Song', if that's not about writing poems, then I don't know what is.

Sam Hunt, 2009

I like being this little bit older.
Given me more time to see the reason
every body has their season,
the shape of their cross on their shoulder.

I like being this little bit sadder.
Always thought it would last forever
and mostly funny if not clever,
the first to fall off the ladder.

Older, sadder - but wiser, never,
not on these heron legs, no:
that's when I say I got to go
hit the road. Which goes on forever.

Sam Hunt

acknowledgements

PHOTO CREDITS

Pages 6/7: Jane Ussher
Page 17: Clifton Firth
Page 24, 26: Betty Hunt
Page 37: Meg Campbell
Page 50, 67: Sara Murphy
Page 57, 135: Sam Hunt
Page 61, 132: Shirley Grace
Page 73: Bill Beavis
Page 74: Bruce Connew
Page 84: John Sepie
Page 101: Prue Ursell
Page 107: Don Higgins
Page 138: John Savage

For some photographs used in this book we have been unable to establish the name of the photographer or the copyright holder. If you are the copyright holder of any photograph used for which clearance has not been obtained, please contact Craig Potton Publishing and we will attempt to remedy the situation.

Sam Hunt at the Portobello Pub (1978) is reproduced with permission from Robin White. From the collection of the Dunedin Art Gallery.

Craig Potton Publishing is grateful to the following authors and publishers for granting permission to reproduce these poems:

'Letter to Sam Hunt', 'Jerusalem Blues 2', 'Inscription' and 'Kumara Poem'; reproduced with permission of Dr Paul Millar, Literary Advisor to the James K. Baxter Trust.

'Salute to a Friend' by Meg Campbell, 'Why don't you talk to me?', 'Drinking Horn' and 'Old Lady Dying'; reproduced with permission of Alistair Te Ariki Campbell.

'Poem for Magda' from *Building*, The Caxton Press, Christchurch, 1963; reproduced with permission of Gordon Challis.

'No Time Ago'; reproduced from *Complete Poems 1904–1962* by E. E. Cummings, edited by George J. Firmage, with permission of W. W. Norton & Company. Copyright © 1991 by the Trustees for the E. E. Cummings Trust and George James Firmage.

'Superstition'; reproduced with permission of Pia Glover and the Denis Glover Literary Estate.

'Flood'; reproduced with permission of Random House New Zealand and the Estate of Hone Tuwhare. Copyright and publishing rights are held by Rob Tuwhare on behalf of the Estate of Hone Tuwhare, email: honetuwharepoetry@gmail.com